TOM
DALEY

ULTIMATE
SPORTS HEROES

TOM
DALEY

GOING FOR GOLD

DINO

First published by Dino Books in 2021,
an imprint of Bonnier Books UK,
The Plaza, 535 King's Road, London SW10 0SZ
Owned by Bonnier Books,
Sveavägen 56, Stockholm, Sweden

🅓 @dinobooks
www.bonnierbooks.co.uk

© Dino Books
Written by Melanie Hamm
Cover illustration by Bruce Huang

Paperback ISBN: 9781789463033
E-book ISBN: 9781789464382

British Library cataloguing-in-publication data:
A catalogue record for this book is available from the British Library.

Printed and bound in Great Britain by Clays Lltd, Elcograf S.p.A.

1 3 5 7 9 10 8 6 4 2

For my parents

TABLE OF CONTENTS

CHAPTER 1 – **BUDAPEST BRILLIANCE** 8

CHAPTER 2 – **WATER BABY** 12

CHAPTER 3 – **THE OTHER POOL** 18

CHAPTER 4 – **DON'T LOOK BEHIND YOU!** 27

CHAPTER 5 – **AGAIN!** 33

CHAPTER 6 – **PETER PAN** 40

CHAPTER 7 – **MEDALS, MEDALS, MEDALS!** 49

CHAPTER 8 – **REACH FOR THE STARS** 60

CHAPTER 9 – **POCKET ROCKET** 69

CHAPTER 10 – **TEN METRES** .77

CHAPTER 11 – **GROWTH SPURT** 83

CHAPTER 12 – **REBUILDING** 91

CHAPTER 13 – **SHEFFIELD** 95

CHAPTER 14 – **WORLD SERIES** 102

CHAPTER 15 – **AMBITION** 108

CHAPTER 16 – **BEIJING** 113

CHAPTER 17 – **A NEW CHAPTER** 121

CHAPTER 18 – **ROME** 128

CHAPTER 19 – **TRAGEDY** 135

CHAPTER 20 – **REDIVE** 143

CHAPTER 21 – **SPLASH!** 153

CHAPTER 22 – **THE FIREWORK** 159

CHAPTER 23 – **MORE THAN DIVING** 167

CHAPTER 1

BUDAPEST BRILLIANCE

22 July 2017

Tom Daley could barely breathe as he watched his rival, Chen Aisen, poised on the edge of the platform. It was the final of the men's 10-metre platform event at the World Aquatic Championships in Budapest and the tension around the pool was electric. Tom led Chen by a margin of just 5.7 points, but both divers had one more dive to perform. With so little difference between their scores, anything could happen. Tom swallowed nervously. He could see the determination and focus in his rival's eyes. If the Chinese diver – the Olympic champion –

delivered a spectacular dive, the gold medal could easily slip from Tom's grasp.

The crowd hushed. Chen leapt from the board and into the air, turning a series of elegant somersaults before dropping neatly into the pool. Cheers rang around the auditorium. Tom gulped. It was a spectacular dive. His eyes flicked to the scoreboard: 106.20. A huge score! It would be very hard to beat.

Chen clambered from the pool, grinning. His teammates clustered around him, buzzing with noisy congratulations. Chen didn't even glance at Tom, standing on the top platform. *He thinks he's won,* Tom realised. *They don't think I can beat him. Well. We'll see about that.*

Tom's competitive spark had been lit. Adrenaline surged through him. He knew he would need the dive of his life to beat Chen. But he had nothing to lose. He would give his all in this final dive.

Here goes.

For a fraction of a second, it felt to Tom as though

he was flying, soaring above the pool with his arms stretched out like wings. As gravity started to tug him downwards, he gripped his knees to his chest and tipped into his first somersault. Round and round he spun, suspended in mid-air, faster, faster. As he tumbled out of his final somersault, the only direction was down, down, down, plummeting at top speed towards the shimmering blue pool below.

As Tom hit the water, an explosion of cheers rocked the auditorium. Up in the stands, Tom's mum, Debbie, let out a cry of delight. Tom's husband, Lance, flung his arms into the air, while at the side of the pool, Tom's coach, Jane, jumped up and down for joy and his Great Britain teammates shrieked and whooped.

Tom could hear the cacophony of sound as he kicked back to the surface.

Was it good? It must have been good for the crowd to be cheering like this!

With eyes on the scoreboard, he blinked in disbelief: 106.20 points. The same score as Chen!

It was enough to keep him on top. He had done it. He had beaten the Olympic champion.

Tom ran straight to Jane and gave her a joyful hug. She had supported and believed in him every step of the way. His teammates crowded round, bombarding him with hugs and kisses.

Meanwhile, his amazing mum and his wonderful husband, his most loyal supporters, were hurrying down from the stands, waiting to fling their arms around the new world champion. Tom felt like he was being swept up in a tidal wave of love, pride and support. He couldn't take the smile off his face. The victory was his. But it also belonged to his family, his friends, his teammates, his coach, his physiotherapist, his fans... everyone who had come on this incredible journey with him.

And at just 23, Tom knew he had much, much more to give. This journey wasn't over yet!

CHAPTER 2

WATER BABY

'He's a water baby!' declared the midwife with a smile.

Tom's parents, Rob and Debbie, watched as the midwife carefully dunked their newborn son into a bath of warm water. As his tiny limbs sank into the water, he let out a happy sigh: 'Ooooooh!'

His parents glanced at each other with a grin. Maybe the midwife was right. Maybe their son was a water baby!

The midwife lifted Tom out of the bath, dabbed him gently with a towel, then placed him into his mother's waiting arms.

'It's those big hands and feet,' she explained. 'That's always the sign.'

Smiles lit up Debbie and Rob's faces as they bent over their tiny squirming son. They didn't care how big his hands and feet were. Water baby, or not, he was their first child. They had waited with excitement and joy for nine months, and he was perfect.

Thomas was the name they had agreed on: Thomas Robert Daley.

'Hello there, Tom,' cooed Rob. He could hardly believe that the moment was finally here – 21 May 1994. The birth of his son. It was the happiest day of his life so far.

From Derriford Hospital, Plymouth, Rob and Debs made the short journey back home, where their families were waiting. Their small house in Plymouth was overflowing with family and friends. There were Rob's parents, David and Rose, and Debbie's parents, Jenny and Doug, along with brothers and sisters on both sides and friends eager to meet the new arrival. With his parents looking on proudly, baby Tom was passed from arm to arm, cuddled, kissed, his hands and cheeks stroked.

'Apparently he's a water baby,' joked Rob. 'Because of those big hands and feet.'

'Well, he's a Plymouth baby, so he's got no choice,' laughed Grandad David. 'He'll spend all his time on the beach, just like you did as a child.'

It was true. It was impossible to avoid the sea in Plymouth.

'You'd better teach him to swim as soon as you can,' added Grandma Rose.

'We will,' said Debs. She was already imagining family days out at Bovisand Beach and Firestone Bay. They were so lucky to live near the sea. She couldn't wait to see baby Tom toddling along the beach in the sun and paddling at the water's edge!

Rob and Debs soon settled into parenthood. There was a steady stream of visitors, and little Tom was always the centre of attention. Rob and Debs watched eagerly for his first smile, and once it came, it didn't go away. He was a happy, playful, curious baby, interested in whatever was going on around him. And it turned out his big hands were very useful for grabbing anything and everything – toys, hair, TV remotes... When December came around, he even made a grab for the Christmas tree.

'Oh, Tom, you'll hurt yourself!' squealed Debs in alarm, rushing to pull him away from the tangle of prickly branches and fairy lights. But little Tom was fearless. Every new sight and sound was an excitement, and he did not want to miss out on a thing!

Tom was growing so fast. He was quick to crawl, then to toddle, then to walk. Rob and Debs decided it was time for him to learn to swim so they enrolled him for swimming lessons at their local pool. He loved the pool immediately and he soon splashed his way to a five-metre certificate.

When Tom was two years old, his brother, William, was born. No-one was keener to cuddle the new baby than big brother Tom.

'Careful, Tom!' warned Rob. 'He's only little. You'll squash him!'

With two small boys, Rob and Debs needed a bigger house. They moved to the nearby suburb of Eggbuckland and settled in a house at the top of the hill with a stunning view across the hillside to the misty grey sea beyond. There was a big garden, and as the boys grew, they loved to run around in it, their games getting more and more rowdy as they got bigger.

Ten days before Tom turned five, his second brother, Ben, was born. Tom was more careful with his cuddles this time. He adored his little brother. Squash little Ben? Never! And he was careful that William didn't squash him either.

As predicted by Grandad David – or Grandad Dink, as the boys called him – Tom and his brothers spent lots of time by the water. Tom loved sports. At school, St Edward's, he was learning judo, tennis and squash. But he was never happier than when splashing around in the sea or the local pool.

Grandad Dink had a speedboat and Tom loved the thrill of bumping over the waves, the boat half in the water, half in the air.

'Can I steer?' he begged his grandpa.

'When you're older,' grinned Grandad Dink. 'Seven is too young to be a skipper. Wait till you're 70, like me!'

Tom laughed. 'Will you make it go faster?'

'Aren't you scared?' asked his grandpa, although he knew the answer already.

'No!' Tom grinned. 'Faster, Grandad! Faster!'

He clung on tight as Grandad Dink turned the steering wheel sharply and sent the little boat curving round in a loop, slicing through the water and sending a great arc of spray into the sky. It was like they were flying!

'Fast enough for you?'

'Awesome!' Tom grinned, then he spoke the words his grandfather always expected. 'Again!'

CHAPTER 3

THE OTHER POOL

Tom and William usually took swimming lessons at their local pool, but Rob had seen a poster for a Saturday Fun Session at Central Park Pool, just outside Plymouth city centre. He knew the boys would enjoy a morning of messing around in the water. So he and Debs packed the car with towels, trunks, inflatables and three noisy, excitable boys.

Once inside, the boys were off, jostling each other through the turnstiles to get to the changing rooms, swinging their swim bags, towels trailing along the corridor. Rob and Debbie smiled at each other. It wasn't just one water baby they had; it was three!

Central Park did not disappoint. The pool was vast and bright, with colourful bunting strung from the ceiling. Spotlights beamed down and music was pumping from hidden speakers. Children of all ages were shouting and laughing, splashing and playing games. With a whoop, William darted towards the inviting blue water, and his parents followed, with little Ben toddling between them.

'Are you coming, Tom?' asked Rob.

Tom had stopped. He had turned away from the hubbub of the main pool and was peering across the walkway at a second pool, glowing brilliant blue under the lights. At the end were a series of diving boards, starting low and getting higher and higher. The highest was taller than a house. Tom watched, transfixed, as a teenage girl climbed the steps to the top platform and prepared to dive. He held his breath as she walked to the end of the board, stopping at the very end. *She's going to fall,* he thought. *It's so high!* But she didn't. She balanced on the edge for a few seconds then leapt into the air, flipped upside down and plunged towards the water, arms first, landing with the smallest of splashes.

Tom let out his breath. *Wow!* After a second, the girl came back to the surface. There was a huge grin on her face. A group of other kids, sitting on the poolside and standing on the lower boards, clapped. Tom wanted to clap too. He couldn't believe she'd dared to jump from so high. He hoped she would do it again!

'Tom?' Rob appeared beside him. 'What's up?'

'Can I learn to do that?' Tom pointed at the diving pool where another kid was jumping from a springboard. 'Please!'

Rob looked down at his son. Tom's eyes were shining. His whole body was quivering with excitement. Together they watched as another young diver climbed up to the highest platform, then jumped into the pool below.

'Looks pretty scary to me, mate,' said Rob.

'*It looks awesome,*' said Tom. 'Please can I try?'

Rob smiled. 'If you really want to.'

Tom flung his arms around his dad's waist. 'Thanks, Dad!'

***

Rob kept his promise. He booked five diving sessions for Tom and Will – who didn't want to be left out.

Tom was fizzing with excitement as he and Will joined the other beginners at the side of the diving pool. While echoing shrieks and splashes made a constant din in the main pool, this pool was quiet. The water was flat and undisturbed, like a mirror. Tom was desperate to jump in and ripple the perfectly still water!

He gazed up at the highest platform, supported by a huge white pillar. From close up, it seemed even higher. His dad had been right, it *did* look a bit scary. Scary and exciting! He imagined himself walking slowly to the edge and leaping into the air, like a bird taking flight...

'Welcome, everyone!' Tom was called back to earth by the voice of the instructor. 'My name is Sam. I'll be teaching you to dive over the next few weeks. Now, have any of you dived before?'

There was silence. 'Well, you're in luck,' Sam continued. 'You'll be learning in one of the best diving pools in the country.' She pointed to the highest platform. 'There aren't many pools with a 10-metre platform!'

The eyes of the class swivelled to stare up at the top board, towering up above them.

'Can we dive off that today?' asked one kid.

'No,' smiled Sam. 'Not for a long time. Ten metres is higher than two double-decker buses. Only experienced divers can jump from that height. We'll just be using the springboards today.'

Even the springboards looked pretty high, Tom thought. The biggest one was as tall as the ceiling at home.

'How high are they?' he asked.

'The highest is three metres,' said Sam. 'But before we start on those, you'll be diving from the poolside.'

Tom couldn't help feeling a little bit relieved.

Sam was standing on the edge of the pool. 'Now, the most important part of the dive is how you launch yourself. You need to get speed and height.'

She demonstrated, launching herself as far as she could out over the water before hitting the surface with a small splash.

'Did you see? My hands went in first and I kept my body really straight. In some dives, you land feet first, but you're still keeping your body super straight. Imagine you're a knife, cutting through the water.'

'What if we don't land hands first?'

'It's going to hurt,' grinned Sam. 'Hands or feet, team, that's what we want to see.'

By now, Tom and Will were itching to get into the water. But Sam had one more golden rule. 'Keep your eyes open until you hit the water, please, everyone,' she told them. 'Close your eyes and you will lose control, which is dangerous.'

Tom gulped. 'What if we forget to close our eyes and they explode when we hit the water?'

Sam laughed. 'Don't worry, your eyes will shut by themselves,' she reassured him. 'Think about when someone splashes you.'

'Like this!' Will sent a shower of spray in the direction of his brother.

'Stop it!' said Sam sternly. But what she'd said was true. Tom's eyes clamped shut before he told them to and before Will's splash reached them. His brain knew exactly what to do!

'Now, let's give all that a go, shall we?' Sam motioned them to the poolside.

Tom, Will and the rest of the group practised standing, just as Sam had shown them on the poolside, shifting their weight in order to fly higher and further into the air. Tom found the higher he went, the faster he plunged into the water. He loved the tingling feeling when his hands hit the surface of the pool, followed by his arms and his head. Once he touched the water, the rest of him was pulled under with a swoosh. He didn't have to do anything, but his body felt full of energy and power as it shot through the water. It felt so exciting!

He looked over at Will. His brother's eyes were gleaming and he was grinning from ear to ear. He could tell Will was enjoying it as much as he was.

After practising dives from poolside, it was time to try the springboard. 'Remember, we want minimal splashing. We want to slip into the water and disturb it as little as possible. And jump as far out from the board as you can, please. I don't want anyone hitting themselves on the board.'

The springboard looked easy – but it wasn't. When Tom jumped, the board sprang back too with so much force that it sent him tumbling into the water, arms and legs flailing. He tried again. This time when he tried to bounce, the board simply stopped moving and, once again, he lost his footing. The wobbling board seemed to have a mind of its own!

But Will didn't seem to have the same problem. It was like he and the springboard were thinking the same thing. Tom watched his brother bounce once, twice, three times – getting higher and higher each time, before propelling himself forward into a dive. Tom frowned. Will was two years younger. How come he was finding it easy? It wasn't fair!

'Okay, session over, team,' called Sam. 'We'll do some more springboard practice next week.'

I'll get it right next week, Tom thought to himself. *If Will can do it, so can I!*

CHAPTER 4

DON'T LOOK BEHIND YOU!

To Tom's frustration, the springboard wasn't the only thing his little brother was better at. Every week, Sam taught them something new – back jumps, tucks, pikes – and Will seemed to pick up everything faster than Tom.

It was so annoying to always be behind! And Will was fearless too. He threw himself into every dive without seeming nervous at all. Tom felt scared before every single dive – particularly the ones where he had to jump off the poolside backwards.

'Don't look behind you!' Sam would shout, but

Tom couldn't help it. He hated not being able to see where he was jumping.

But it was all worth it for the feeling of pride when he mastered a new dive.

With Sam's encouragement, Tom, Will and the rest of the group were working their way through the first of the official diving certificates. The dives started simple and Sam was strict about getting every tiny detail right:

'Tom, point your feet!'

'Will, jump higher!'

'Ankles together, boys.'

'Keep your backs straight, everyone. One straight line from head to toe. Trust me, if you get the small things right now, they'll be automatic by the time you come to do more complicated dives.'

Rob never missed watching a session, and every time the boys brought home a new certificate, he laminated it and put it in a special folder.

'It's only a piece of paper, Dad.' Tom pulled a face. 'You don't need to do that!'

But secretly he was pleased. He loved the feeling of getting better every session. And Will was no longer leaving him behind either. Tom was catching up fast!

Tom couldn't wait to be doing the amazing dives that he saw the older divers doing, leaping off the higher platforms, doing somersaults and twists in mid-air. He found out that the teenage girl that he had seen on the morning they had first come to Central Park Pool was called Brooke Graddon, and she was one of the most confident divers. Tom loved to watch her running along the platform and flinging herself into crazy acrobatic positions as if it were the easiest thing in the world. He wanted to be able to fly through the air like that!

As the weeks went by, the group learned about the five types of dive: forward, back, reverse, inward and twist. There was also a sixth type, called armstand dives, which were only ever done off the platform.

'Let's not worry about those for now,' Sam told

them. 'Some of you may learn them in a few years' time.'

The group started with forward and back dives, which were the easiest. Next they moved on to inward dives, jumping off the side of the pool with their backs to the water then flipping forward in mid-air to plunge headfirst into the water.

Tom's heart pounded in his chest every time it was his turn. He knew if he didn't jump far enough, he would hit his head on the side of the pool – Sam had warned them of this! But once he was in the air, his fear turned to adrenaline. He flipped over and plummeted towards the pool, happiness bursting through him as he surged through the water, letting momentum carry him down, down, down.

'Excellent, Tom,' said Sam. 'Well done, everyone. Now, who would like to have a go at some somersaults? I think you're ready.'

Somersaults? Tom's ears pricked up. This would be fun!

Sam explained the basics. Push off strongly. Jump

as far and high as possible. Keep looking forward – never look down. Let's give it a go!' she said.

Tom's legs trembled as he stood waiting for his turn. He watched the other kids try – it looked so hard! By the time he was standing on the end of the board, Tom's whole body was shaking. He didn't want to do it anymore! *He couldn't do it!*

Sam could see his nerves. 'You can do it, Tom,' she said. 'You'll be fine.'

She was right. Leaping off the board and turning somersaults in mid-air was the best feeling ever. Time seemed to slow down. While he was spinning, Tom felt like he would never land. He really was flying!

'Great effort, Tom!' cried Sam. 'Next time, try picking a spot on the ceiling and keep looking at it. That'll give you more control. And see if you can tuck your knees more tightly into your chest.'

He did – and found himself spinning even faster. By making tiny adjustments, he was able to change the somersault. It was like magic!

'Tom! Keep away from the board!' called Sam, sounding alarmed. 'You don't want to hit your head!'

But, spinning through the air, Tom felt fearless. He couldn't remember why he had felt so scared standing on the edge of the board. How strange it was. Like his body and mind were thinking two different things and having an argument about it. If only Tom could teach his brain that his body knew what it was doing. If only his mind could trust his body, then he knew his nerves would simply float away!

CHAPTER 5

AGAIN!

It was Saturday morning and Andy Banks, the head coach at Plymouth Diving Club, was in his office as usual. The phone on the desk rang and Andy reached to pick it up. Sam was on the line, calling from the diving pool.

'Sam? Is something wrong?'

'Are you free now? I'd like you to come and see something. Or rather, someone.'

That was intriguing. 'I'll be right down,' Andy told her.

He hurried to poolside where Sam was waiting. There was a big grin on her face.

'What's going on?' he asked.

Sam gestured to a small boy, standing nervously by the one-metre springboard. 'This is Tom Daley. I've been wanting you to see Tom dive for weeks now. I think he's got something special.'

Andy stared at Tom, who responded by running away from the board and hiding behind a pillar.

'Tom, will you come and show us your new dive?' Sam asked, walking over to him.

Tom was shaking with nerves and tears were rolling down his cheeks.

'What's wrong, Tom?' she asked with concern. 'You've done this dive before.'

'I want to go home,' Tom said in a quavering voice. 'I don't want to dive anymore.'

From the sidelines, Andy frowned. What was going on?

'Tom's been working on the forward double somersault and tuck,' Sam told Andy. 'Tom, you can do this. You know you can.'

How had he done it before? Suddenly Tom

couldn't believe that he had managed to turn two somersaults in mid-air. Plus a tuck. And land the right way up. How had he not messed up and hurt himself? It must have been luck! He *definitely* wouldn't be able to do it again. He could see himself landing in the water with a painful smack. Even the thought of perching on the end of the wobbling springboard made him feel sick.

'I'm not doing it. I'm not diving ever again,' he told Sam, and then ran over to where Rob was sitting in the stands.

His dad put a comforting arm around him. 'You want to go home, Tom?'

Tom nodded miserably. 'Yes.'

Andy Banks watched as they left the pool. Then he turned to Sam. 'This kid will never be a diver,' he declared. 'Not with that attitude. If he gets scared on the one-metre springboard, what will he be like on the higher boards?' He put his hands on his hips and frowned. 'Is this the first time he's run off?'

Sam shook her head. 'He gets nervous. But he always, always does the dive in the end. He'll be back. You'll see.'

But Andy was already at the exit. 'I've seen enough, thanks, Sam.'

Meanwhile, in the changing rooms, Tom scrambled into his clothes and flung his trunks and towel into his swim bag. Suddenly nothing was more important than getting out of here, as quickly as he could! As he rushed to the foyer, Rob enveloped him in one of his big, warm bear hugs, and then together they walked to the car. Tom took a big, deep breath. Outside, away from the pool, with his dad beside him, he already felt calmer.

'Now, you're sure you don't want to go back?' said Rob gently as he shut the car door.

Tom's gaze was fixed straight ahead. 'I don't want to go back.'

'Absolutely sure?' Rob fastened his seat belt.

'Yes.'

'Absolutely, totally sure?' Rob turned the key in

the ignition.

Tom turned to look at his dad and Rob saw a flicker of hesitation in his son's eyes. He knew what was coming next...

'Um... Can we go back, please?' Tom said in a quiet voice. 'I want to do the dive.'

Five minutes later, Tom was back in his trunks, back on the poolside. Inside him, nerves battled against excitement. Before, nerves had triumphed, but now it was excitement that was winning. His whole body tingled as he imagined spinning through the air and plunging through the water at rocket speed. Why had he been so scared?

'Okay, mister. You're up,' said Sam.

Tom darted over to the springboard. He did the special 'hurdle' step that Sam had taught him. Then he gave a single, strong bounce and used the power of the springboard to launch himself into the air. For a moment, he felt as light as a feather. He pulled his legs into his chest, then he spun once, twice, before releasing his legs and letting the weight of his body send him falling feet first into the pool. He made sure to keep his toes pointed and his arms pinned to his sides. There was a short, sharp *splosh* as his body hit the water, and then he was sucked under in a whirl of bubbles.

After a few seconds, he stopped sinking. For a brief moment, he hung in the water near the bottom of the pool, before kicking his legs and propelling himself back to the surface, bubbles fizzing in his ears.

'Well done,' cried Sam. 'That was excellent, Tom!'

If only Andy had seen it, she thought with frustration.

Tom felt a warm glow of pride. So far, he was the only person in the class who had managed this dive. Tom was sure that Will would have mastered it too, if he'd been there. But his brother wasn't coming to diving lessons anymore. He preferred playing football and rugby with his classmates. And without Will, Tom was leaving the rest of the class far behind. Everyone else was spinning and coming out the wrong way, falling head first towards the water. Tom wasn't sure how, but he knew exactly when to straighten out. He always timed it so that his body would be pointing directly downwards. Unlike the other kids, he hardly ever landed on his belly or on his back.

'It's like you've got an inner compass,' Sam told him. 'You seem to know instinctively where your body is when you're in mid-air. You've very lucky, Tom. Few people have that skill. It can't be taught.'

It didn't stop Tom being scared, though. He knew anything could happen if he lost concentration. He was terrified of landing badly or hitting himself on the board. But right now, his fears were far, far away.

'Can I do it again?' he asked. 'Please?'

CHAPTER 6

PETER PAN

The dives Tom was learning were getting more and more complicated. Sam was introducing half twists, twists, backward somersaults, reverse dives. She marvelled at how advanced Tom was for his age. He listened carefully to all her instructions and was good at putting her advice into practice. He was jumping from the three-metre board now, and Sam knew it wouldn't be long before he was ready to start diving in junior competitions.

At last, head coach Andy had to admit that Sam was right: young Tom had something special. But he remained worried about how nervous Tom got

– he would still get scared and refuse to dive. If Tom was going to compete against other divers, Andy knew he would need a strategy to help him to overcome his fears...

'Do you know the story of Peter Pan?' Andy asked him.

Tom nodded. He loved stories. At home, he was reading Harry Potter with his mum.

'Well, you remember how the Darling children learn how to fly?'

'Yes! They think happy thoughts,' Tom replied.

'Exactly,' smiled Andy. 'And you need to do the same. Whenever you feel scared, remind yourself that if *you* think happy, positive thoughts, you'll be able to do it. Thinking positive is what will allow you to fly!'

'I'll try,' said Tom.

'Good. Anything is possible, Tom. You just need to believe you can do it.'

* * *

Tom was bursting with excitement at the idea of competing – and he didn't have long to wait. In April 2003, a month before his ninth birthday, the National Novice Competition would be held at Central Park Pool. Thirty divers would be taking part in Tom's age group. Tom's whole family – Rob, Debs, Will and Ben – would be there to cheer him on.

Tom had spent weeks learning about diving competitions from Sam and Andy. There were three sections to each competition: prelims, semi-finals and the final. Each diver would perform six dives, which was called their 'list'. The list had to be given to the judges in advance.

Back home, Tom explained it to Rob and Debs.

'You can't decide to do different dives on the day – you'd lose lots of points,' he said. 'And the scoring is really complicated. If you do an easy dive really well, you'll get good scores from the judges. But then the scores get multiplied by the tariff. And if your dive is easy, the tariff won't be very high.'

'Hang on, love, what's the tariff?' asked Debs.

Tom grinned. 'Every dive has a "tariff", which shows how difficult it is. The easiest dive has a tariff of 1.2 and the hardest is 4.8.'

Debs and Rob smiled at each other. The scoring was pretty confusing, but they loved to see Tom's face light up as he explained it.

'There are five judges and they all give a score from zero to ten,' Tom continued. 'Ten means it's perfect.'

'And zero means you've messed it up. Like Tom will!' Will cut in, giggling.

Tom blew a raspberry. 'So how many points is *this* dive worth?'

He hurled himself head-first at his brother, and they tumbled backwards onto the sofa, laughing and tickling. Little Ben scrambled on top, and Rob and Debs knew the diving explanation was over.

Central Park Pool was packed on the day of the Novice Competition. The divers and their families had travelled from all over the country to take part.

Excited chatter and the shrill squeals of children echoed around the pool, bouncing off the tiled walls and the glassy surface of the water.

Tom stared down at the familiar diving pool. It was completely still, like a luminous blue block. He felt a shiver of excitement; he couldn't wait to break the stillness with a turbo-charged dive. Or a dive bomb. That would be cool! But a dive bomb wouldn't win him any points. And without any points, he wouldn't have a chance of winning the gleaming silver trophy that was on display beside the judges' table. Tom wanted the trophy more than he'd wanted anything EVER.

Tom ran through his list of dives in his head. He had practised all six dives over and over with Sam till the movements were automatic. The details whirled about in his mind: point toes, arch back, arms straight, bend deep, jump high, legs straight, tuck tight. He knew the judges would be looking at his starting position, take-off, flight and entry into the water. He must get the correct arm position for every dive or points would be deducted. Every spin and twist needed to be complete – or more points would be lost. He felt a cold trickle of fear run from his head to his toes. There was so much to remember!

When the announcer called his name, Tom walked to the side of the springboard. There was no going back now. Panic was washing through him like a wave, ready to overwhelm him.

No, Tom told himself. He summoned his happy Peter Pan thoughts. *I can do this. I want to do this!*

The noise of the crowd died down. Tom positioned himself on the end of the board, his back to the water, and stretched his arms to the sky. He bounced a couple of times, higher, higher, before letting his feet leave the board. As he flipped into his first somersault, he focused on a spot on the ceiling. Rotating into his second somersault, his gaze returned magnetically to the same spot. Finally, his inner compass told him it was the moment to shoot his legs out straight and drop down into the water, twisting to land feet first, facing away from the board.

Splash!

As Tom's head plunged under the water, the noises of the room were suddenly muffled. A grin spread over his face. It wasn't his most difficult dive, but he knew he had done it well. Kicking strongly, he hurried to the surface where Sam's thumbs-up told him he was right. A good performance! A flying start!

With 30 divers competing, the competition was a long one. Up on the big electronic scoreboard, the score flashed up after every round of dives. With his strong first dive, Tom started near the top of the leaderboard. It was agonising watching his name slip down at the end of a round, when other divers had performed better. But it gave him the motivation he needed to do an even better dive next time.

'First or last, it doesn't matter,' his dad had said. But Tom *really* wanted a medal. His heart was in his mouth by the time he went into the final round. He dived well – but would his competitors dive better? Would their dives be harder and have higher tariffs? Would they score more points?

'Relax, Tom,' whispered Sam beside him. 'You've done your best. You can't do any more than that.'

At last the final diver had dived. For an instant, the electronic scoreboard went blank, before the scores flashed up in bright red digits. Tom's eyes were drawn straight to his own name: *Thomas Daley. 103.80 points.* He was second! He had won a silver medal!

Rob punched the air.

Debs let out a whoop of delight.

Little Ben clapped.

Even Will gave a celebratory fist pump.

'Well done, Tom. Brilliant job,' cried Sam, patting him on the back. 'You've gone and won a medal in your first competition!'

Tom grinned from ear to ear as he joined the gold and bronze medallists on the podium. Hearing the cheers of the crowd ringing around the pool and feeling the weight of the medal around his neck were the best feelings in the world.

But his eyes kept being drawn to the gleaming silver trophy.

Next time... Next time he wanted to be first!

CHAPTER 7

MEDALS, MEDALS, MEDALS!

The junior competition squad at Plymouth Diving Club was nicknamed 'the Weenies', and following his brilliant performance at the National Novice Competition, Andy and Sam decided to put Tom in the squad. At just nine, Tom was the youngest diver on the team. He would be competing against much older kids and teenagers. But he was easily as good as the older kids; no-one who saw him dive could doubt his talent.

Tom was now training three times a week, as well as attending weekend training camps, provided by World Class Start, a training programme for young divers with the potential to become international athletes one day. Here the trainers used other sports, like ballet and gymnastics, climbing and even abseiling, to give the young divers strength, flexibility and build their courage and confidence.

As the dives that Tom was learning became more and more complicated, Sam introduced him to the rig: a harness suspended from a frame by strong elastic cords. Strapped into the harness, he could perform somersaults, twists, pikes and tucks.

'It's a less dangerous way to learn complex dives,' Sam explained.

Tom and his fellow divers used a converted squash court as their 'dry land' training area. In addition to the rig, there were 'dry boards' — springboards that launched over a thick, bouncy crash mat — trampolines, and a foam pit, which was a pool filled with foam bricks.

It felt weird at first, jumping onto things that weren't water.

'Is it going to hurt?' Tom asked, looking nervously

at the foam pit.

'Not as much jumping into the pool,' Sam laughed. 'Landing on water is very hard on your body. Landing on foam is much gentler. Try it!'

She was right. The foam blocks looked uncomfortable, but they squished softly when he landed. The sharp, tingling feeling of his skin hitting the water was gone.

'If you go on to compete at an advanced level, most of your training will be on dry land,' Sam told him. 'Especially when you start diving off the 10-metre platform!'

Tom grinned. The 10-metre board was his ultimate goal. At every session, he stared up at it with a mixture of fear and excitement. He knew he wouldn't be allowed to dive from the top platform till he was a teenager. And Tom knew there was a lot to master first...

The five-metre platform.

The seven-metre platform.

Reverse and inward dives.

Everyone at Central Park Pool was amazed by Tom's progress. In competition, he was getting used to winning. His bedroom was filling up with medals, gold, silver and bronze. In fact, Rob had hammered hooks into the ceiling, so they could hang side by side. When Tom opened his window, they jingled against one another like wind chimes!

Little Ben was fascinated by the gleaming, tinkling medals.

'Are they real?' he asked.

'No,' grinned Tom, biting into a medal like he had seen athletes do on TV. 'Even the Olympic medal isn't *pure* gold.'

Ben looked disappointed.

'Okay, wait, I'll show you something that's *really* cool,' said Tom. 'This is my chammy, signed by Pete Waterfield!' The Olympic diver was one of his heroes. 'Look! Dad took a picture when I met him in Southampton!'

Little Ben took hold of the chammy. He looked confused. 'Sh-ammy? What is it?'

'You've seen me drying myself before I dive? I use a little towel like this, called a chamois. Or chammy. It's so I don't slip on the board.'

Ben's face lit up. 'Oh! I saw you do that! Then you throw it over the edge of the board!'

Tom smiled. It was cool that his youngest brother was interested in diving.

'So you'll come and cheer for me at the Nationals?' Tom asked. He would be competing in the British Championship the following week, his first ever national championship event.

Ben grinned and squealed, 'Yes!' He loved to watch his big brother dive.

Rob checked the camcorder for the umpteenth time. Recording. It was definitely recording. He didn't want to miss a second of his son's first national championship competition!

Over the past few years, Rob had been to every single one of Tom's training sessions at Central Park Pool. He had seen Tom dive from the one-metre board, then the three-metre board, then the towering five- and seven-metre platforms. He had seen Tom turn his first somersault, then two, and finally, two-and-a-half somersaults. He was continually astounded by the incredible feats his 10-year-old son could achieve, flipping and twisting and spinning with the grace and control of an acrobat. But still he couldn't help thinking how tiny Tom looked, standing all the way up there on the edge of the seven-metre platform. Tiny... and scared.

Perched on the very edge of the seven-metre platform, gripping the board with his toes, Tom was scared. He was petrified. This was the biggest event of his life, in front of the biggest audience. What if he tumbled off the board? What if he hit the platform with his head while he spun? What if he lost control in the air and landed on his back? Tom pushed the thoughts away. What would Andy say? *Think Peter Pan. Think happy thoughts in order to fly!*

The crowd hushed and Tom shot the quickest

of glances at the stands where his family were watching. *Please let it be a good dive!*

His first dive was one of his simplest: a front two-and-a-half somersaults with pike.

Rising onto his tiptoes, Tom summoned all his courage and launched himself up and forward, jumping well clear of the dreaded platform with its deadly, sharp edge. Hovering for a split second in mid-air, he bent in two, clamping his legs to his chest, gripping them tightly with his hands to make the pike position. Then he spun elegantly downwards, finally releasing his arms and legs and plunging into the water, as quick and straight as an arrow. The whole dive was over in less than two seconds.

Through the gurgle of the water, Tom heard the cheers of the crowd. As he bobbed up to the surface, his eyes, along with everyone else's, flew to the scoreboard. *Yes!* The judges had given him good scores. Andy and Sam were beaming at the side of the pool. Up in the stands, Rob was bouncing with delight, while trying to keep his camcorder steady.

Tom's thoughts were already on his next dive. As he sat and watched the rest of the divers complete their first-round dives, his whole body tingled with anticipation and nerves. He wished he could go straight up there and get it over with. Watching and waiting felt like agony!

Eventually it was Tom's turn to dive again. More good scores. The judges liked his inward two-and-a-half somersaults with tuck. A harder dive than the last one.

A back one-and-a-half somersaults with tuck followed. More points.

Then a reverse one-and-a-half somersaults piked. So far, so good.

Then a back half somersault. Another good score.

Finally came the armstand somersault, the last dive on Tom's list. As Tom leant forward and shifted the weight of his body onto his hands, slowly raising his feet off the ground till he was upside down, it was Debs' turn to feel her stomach flipping. Her small son was balanced perilously on the very edge of the platform with his back to the water – she almost couldn't bear to watch!

But Tom's control was total. Quickly and decisively, he flew off the end of the platform, through the air, spinning neatly then dropping into the pool below with a short, sharp splash that echoed round the room. Debs released her breath and joined the applause. Another excellent dive.

But as usual, Tom would need to wait till the end of the round when every diver had dived, before knowing if his performance had been good enough for a medal. The competition among the Under-18s had been fierce so far; Tom was competing against teenagers up to seven years older than him!

Tom watched as the other divers spun and flipped, some from three metres, some from five. Along with the rest of the crowd, he cheered each dive – and felt a pang of sympathy for the divers who made mistakes. He knew how badly they would be feeling. Engrossed in the drama of each dive, he had almost forgotten that these were his competitors!

As the final diver left the pool and the last ripples ebbed away, once again, the pool was still and flat like a sheet of glass. Tom sat beside Sam and Andy as the final calculations were being made by the judges. The suspense was painful. In seconds, the results would be revealed – wait, there they were, in glowing neon:

Tom Daley: third place! Bronze!

Andy and Sam were on their feet, flinging their arms around him, whooping for joy. 'This makes you the youngest ever under-18s medallist!' Sam cried. 'Congratulations, Tom! And you're the winner in your age group.'

'Wait, wait!' Andy's eyes were back on the scoreboard. 'Tom is eighth overall – including the seniors!'

Tom blinked. 'Seriously?' He was only seven places behind the winner.

'It's an incredible achievement, Tom,' said Sam.

'We're so proud of you!'

Of course, she wasn't the only one to feel this way. Up in the stands, Rob wept tears of pride. Beside him, Debs shared his delight. As they watched Tom step onto the podium to collect his medal, a tiny figure beside the teenage gold and silver medallists, they hugged each other, and Will and Ben, for joy.

CHAPTER 8

REACH FOR
THE STARS

'Daaaaad!' Tom flung himself into the front seat of the campervan next to Rob and slammed the door shut behind him. 'Please turn off that stupid horn! Why do you always have to embarrass me?!'

It was four o'clock on Friday afternoon, at the end of Tom's first week at secondary school. As his schoolmates streamed out of the gates of Eggbuckland Community College, the last thing Tom wanted was for his classmates to see his dad arriving to collect him in a bright green van with the loudest, most ridiculous Dixie horn in the entire universe. His new friends were laughing their heads off and Tom was wishing that he and more importantly, his dad – would disappear.

Rob silenced the din of Dixie horn. 'It's just a bit of fun,' he grinned. 'Cheers me up, anyway.'

Tom sulked. 'I thought we'd agreed I was going to walk home. It's bad enough that everyone knows we go caravanning, without them thinking I'm in the circus.'

The Daleys went caravanning at Newquay most weekends, when Tom didn't have training.

'I'm picking you up so we can get on the road straight away,' said Rob. 'It seems reasonable to me, mate.'

But it didn't seem reasonable to Tom. He had just spent a week trying his hardest to fit in. Up till now, it had been going pretty well. But now he would be a laughing stock, thanks to his dad and his stupid comedy horn.

'Are you going to sulk all the way to Newquay, Tom?' asked Rob.

No reply.

'I'll take that as a yes. I'm going to stick The Vengaboys on then. Sit back. Enjoy.'

The sound of 'We Like to Party' boomed from the speakers and Tom sunk even lower in his seat. Why, oh why, was his dad so embarrassing?!

But by the time they reached Newquay, Tom's worries had disappeared, drowned out by his dad's beloved Europop. It had been a pretty good week, after all. He liked his new class, 7N. He liked his teachers. He had made friends with a cool group of kids, Sophie, Alex, Nikita and Harriet. He had sat next to Sophie at the back of the geography class and they had laughed and joked around throughout the lesson. He had a feeling they were going to be good mates. Plus, the September sun was shining and a weekend of swimming, biking, tennis and cricket lay ahead. Tom and his brothers loved to play outdoors and Watergate Bay, near Newquay, was their all-time favourite place to be.

Tom wasn't disappointed. The campsite pool was sparkling in the evening sunshine and he was the first to dive in. He was training five days a week now, but he still couldn't get enough of the water!

'So who's looking forward to karaoke?' asked Rob as he prepared the BBQ that night. Karaoke at the clubhouse was a regular Saturday night event, and the highlight of Rob's weekend. He made sure that his family were always there.

Tom rolled his eyes. Karaoke was yet another way that his dad was embarrassing! Rob would always perform as Elvis Presley – always. But at least this time there would be no-one from school to witness it.

'You think you know what I've got planned,' Rob said, winking at him. 'But you don't.'

'Dad!' Tom glared at him, but his scowl quickly turned to laughter. He couldn't help it. His dad's enthusiasm for karaoke was infectious.

Saturday passed quickly, with bike rides thought the woods, more swimming and games of tennis. Tom had to admit, he was secretly looking forward to the evening, and Rob's singing surprise.

After dinner, Debbie led the boys to the clubhouse, where the stage was lit up with fairy lights. The room was already crowded. Tom and his brothers jostled each other for seats near the back, while onstage the compere tested the mic.

'Testing, testing...' The mic crackled to life and the compere plucked it from the stand. 'Welcome, one and all! It's kaaaaaraoke night!' She beamed a wide smile at the audience. 'I hope you're all in good voice. Let's raise the roof!'

Tom grinned. One thing was for sure, karaoke night at Watergate Bay was always loud!

But where was Rob?

Three or four singers came forward to perform pop songs with gusto and varying levels of skill before the compere stepped forward with an announcement.

'You know him. You love him. Let's give it up for The King. Yes, *Elvis* is in the building...'

Tom watched as Rob strode onstage, his hips swaying wildly from side to side. He was wearing his full Elvis costume – the white leather flares studded with jewels, gold rings on every finger, plus a puffy black wig. The audience cheered. They loved Rob's routine. It wouldn't be karaoke night without an appearance from Elvis!

Rob seized the mic and in a low, rumbling, Elvis-ish voice said. 'I'm gonna be singin' with someone verrrrry special tonight. Can ya guess who it is?'

Tom giggled. Was his dad going to drag his mum onstage? Surely not! She'd hate it!

'My son Tom. Tom, will you come up here and join your dad – I mean, Elvis.'

Tom's eyebrows shot up his forehead. He gave a squeak of horror. Singing in front of all these people? In front of the rest of his family? No way!

'Tom, I'm beggin' ya,' Elvis continued, in his drawling American accent. 'Don't disappoint the king of rock'n'roll.'

Will and Ben were nudging Tom on either side. 'Go on!'

The stage looked very bright. The mic sounded

very loud. The audience was very big. Tom knew he only had a few seconds to make his mind up – and he didn't want to let his dad down. So he swallowed his fears, summoned his courage and stood up. The crowd cheered him all the way to the stage, until Elvis put up a hand for silence.

'What are you going to sing for us tonight, Tom?' he asked.

Tom gave a small smile. Somehow being onstage didn't feel quite as scary as he'd imagined. What was the worst that could happen? He made a mistake and everyone laughed at him? Maybe that wouldn't be so bad.

'"Reach" by S Club 7, please,' he said.

'Are we doing the dance?' asked Elvis.

Tom's confidence was growing. He rolled his eyes comically, looking at the audience. 'Er, obviously!'

The sound of S Club 7 blared from the speakers. Tom gulped. *Here goes!*

He launched himself into the familiar lyrics. How loud his voice sounded through the microphone!

He sounded like a screeching bat. It wasn't cool – but that didn't matter. It was FUN!

By the time the chorus came, Tom was enjoying himself, and so were the audience. He flung his hand in the air every time he 'reached for the stars' and Elvis copied, his tight leather suit squeaking in protest. The crowd roared with laughter and Tom found himself struggling to sing through his giggles.

When they reached the finale, Elvis flung a big, jewel-studded arm around him and together they flourished their mics in the air. The crowd went wild, whooping and stamping their feet. Tom felt like he'd dived a triple somersault and twist off the seven-metre board!

'Never worry what other people think, Tom,' whispered his dad beneath the din. 'Remember that next time you're on the diving board. Be the best you can be. No-one else's opinion matters.'

Tom smiled. 'Thanks, Dad.'

Rob was right. His diving nerves came from worrying about making mistakes and looking silly.

From now on, he would try to forget everyone else's expectations.

And if the other kids laughed at their bright green van with its Dixie horn... so what?

CHAPTER 9

POCKET ROCKET

'There's a delivery for you, Tom!' shouted Debs from the hallway.

Tom rushed downstairs. His mum was carrying a large box. He wasn't expecting anything – it wouldn't be his birthday for months! What could it be?

'Open it then!' urged Debs.

Tom tore off the tape and pulled back the flaps.

'My Team GB kit!' he cried.

In April 2005, Tom would be taking part in his first international competition, the Aachen Junior International in Germany. Aged just 10, technically he was too young to compete. But Kim White, the performance director at British Swimming, had persuaded the German Swimming Federation to relax the rules. Tom would be diving for Great Britain for the very first time!

'What do you think, Mum?' Tom asked, pulling his GB tracksuit on over his clothes.

Debs grinned. 'You look like a proper sports star, my love.'

He added the GB cap and struck a pose. 'Look, there are T-shirts, shorts, trunks, a drinks bottle... I'm going to wear the tracksuit to training.'

Tom's confidence was high and he was diving better than ever. Sam and Andy had put together an ambitious list of dives for the competition. But they knew how tough the competition would be...

'You mustn't be surprised if you slip down the leaderboard, Tom,' Sam told him. 'It's your first international competition. Don't be surprised if you don't make the final.'

'You'll be competing against the best young

divers in the world,' explained Andy. 'Especially the Chinese team. They're the favourites.'

'Most of all, this is great experience,' added Sam. 'Anything more is a bonus.'

Tom nodded. *Don't expect too much.*

But still... When Tom's competitive streak kicked in, they all knew anything could happen.

***

The karaoke-night confidence booster seemed to be working. Diving in front of a big and buzzing audience, including his parents and Grandma Rose, Tom was on sparkling form. His whole body tingled with excitement and adrenaline as he stood on the platform, waiting to jump. His nerves seemed to have melted away. When he jumped, his body felt weightless, defying gravity to soar through the air, spinning, spinning, spinning, before plunging into the deep blue pool below. The cheers of the crowd rang through his head, resonating through his body, pushing him to jump higher, further, faster.

But this was by far the strongest field Tom had ever competed in. His competitors, from all over the world, were the most focused, talented and experienced he had ever dived against.

Don't be surprised if you don't make the final.

This is great experience.

Anything more is a bonus.

In the end, it was luck that put Tom in the final. The young Russian diver ahead of him made a mistake and slipped down the leaderboard. Thanks to his error, Tom moved up to twelfth position. He had scraped into the final. His first international final!

But against these amazing divers, Tom knew he needed to up his game. He couldn't rely on other divers making mistakes. He needed to be stronger, faster, more precise. He had a spark. But he needed a fire.

Andy and Sam watched as Tom flung himself from the board, his small, compact figure spinning like a Catherine wheel, before slicing neatly into the water. He barely caused a splash. The judged rewarded him with his first ever 9!

With every dive, Tom was rocketing up the leaderboard. At poolside, Andy and Sam looked at each other in astonishment.

'Could he actually *win*?' whispered Sam. 'I've never seen him dive like this!'

'Me neither,' Andy replied. 'It seems like anything is possible with Tom Daley!'

But Tom didn't quite make it to gold. He made an error in his reverse two-and-a-half somersaults and had to settle for silver.

'A silver medal!' Rob wept tears of joy. Debs was close to tears too.

Even Will looked impressed. 'An international silver! Well done, bro!'

'What happened to you up there?' asked Andy. 'It was like you changed gear.'

Tom looked at his feet. 'I guess I just decided to go for it. You said there were no expectations, so I decided to make my own.'

'Feel free to go for it all the time,' joked Sam. 'You're a star, Tom Daley.'

It was official. At just 12, Tom was the second best junior diver in the world. And it wasn't just Sam and Andy who were starting to get excited. There were articles and headlines about Tom in all the newspapers, full of praise and hope about his future:

'One to watch.'

'A brilliant future.'

'A spectacular young talent.'

'A future Olympian.'

Suddenly the eyes of world were on Tom. Almost overnight, from Germany to China, divers all over the globe knew Tom's name. And not just divers... The British media were starting to get interested too. *The Daily Mail* picked him as one of their 'Magnificent Seven' young athletes with potential to win medals at the London 2012 Olympics. Rob filed every newspaper and magazine article about

Tom alongside the diving certificates in his special folder. By now it was full to bursting.

Not long afterwards, Tom's parents had a call from the BBC, who wanted to make a documentary about him. Rob and Debs agreed, allowing the cameras to come into their home, and to follow Tom as he went to training, competed in events and hung out with his family.

Debs preferred not to be on camera but luckily, Tom enjoyed the attention. So did Rob, and he saved some of his best pranks for the cameras. Tom got a shock when his dad's face popped up outside the window of his bedroom on the first floor, waving Tom's lucky monkey.

'Dad!' Tom squealed with surprise then burst out laughing. 'What are you doing up there?'

Rob wobbled on the ladder and pulled a face.

But Tom knew how to deal with his dad's practical jokes. He grinned... and pulled down the blind. 'See you later, Dad!'

Acclaim, newspaper profiles and now TV

documentaries – Tom Daley was fast becoming a name to watch.

CHAPTER 10

TEN METRES

Higher than a house. Higher than a tree. Higher than two double decker buses... Tom had always stared up at the 10-metre diving platform with a mix of fear and excitement.

And now he was standing on top of it. Or rather, he was crouching at the back of it. Right now, fear was winning over excitement. Big time. As he crept slowly forward on his hands and knees, Tom had never ever felt so scared. For every inch that he moved, the board seemed to get narrower and narrower. It felt like he could fall off the side at any moment. Below him, the pool looked like a solid block of blue glass. The thought of jumping made his stomach churn.

'I need a moment,' he called to Andy, below.

'Are you going to stand up?' asked Andy.

Tom thought about it. 'No.'

'Remember Peter Pan,' said Andy. 'Think happy thoughts and you can fly.'

Tom grimaced. Nothing – not Peter Pan, nor Elvis karaoke – could help him now. The platform was simply really, really, *really* high!

'You need to just jump,' said Andy. 'A simple jump. Show yourself it's okay.'

'I'll do it,' replied Tom. 'Just... not yet.'

So he stayed where he was, crouched low on the board. After a few minutes, though, his mind adjusted to the new normal: being way up in the air. He finally felt confident enough to stand up. Then a few minutes after that, he felt secure enough to jump.

Here goes, he thought, and leapt. He raised his arms into the air, pointed his toes, making himself as streamlined as possible, then... *splash!*

'That wasn't so bad, was it?' smiled Andy.

Tom grinned as he returned to the surface. 'Not so bad. I'm going to dive properly this time.'

He climbed the steps back up to the platform then paused to dry his limbs with his chammy. Up here, on the top board, it was more important than ever not to slip!

Then he perched on the end of the board with his back to the pool. He would perform his favourite dive, an inward two-and-a-half somersaults piked. He leapt, feeling the adrenaline surge as his feet left the board. As he flung his arms around his legs and spun, it felt like he was moving in slow motion. Finally he snapped into a vertical position and plunged downwards, hands first. Breaking through the surface of the water, it felt like he was being sucked under by a powerful force. There was barely a splash.

'A rip entry!' Andy clapped his hands together. 'Brilliant!'

Divers aimed for a 'rip entry' on every dive – but only the very best divers achieved it. Instead of a splash, the water made a sound like a piece of paper being ripped apart. The sucking force that Tom had felt was the 'vacuum' – an empty space containing no air and no water – that he had created when his clasped hands pushed through the surface.

'Well done, Tom. So how did that feel?'

Tom swam to the edge of the pool and shook the water from his hair. 'Amazing. Can I dive again?'

Andy nodded. 'One more. It's not safe to dive too much from 10 metres. It puts the body under a lot of strain. Oh, and we're going to have to get you some wrist supports. Your hands take a lot of the impact when you hit the water.'

It was frustrating to have to stop. Flying through the air from 10 metres was exhilarating. But Andy was right. Tom could feel his wrists tingling. They were definitely taking the strain.

'We'll work on your strength in dry-land training,' Andy told him. 'Then we'll build up to six dives per session. No more than that while your bones are still developing.'

Tom's confidence on the 10-metre platform grew with every session. He was hungry to learn and, with the opportunity to hone his technique in the dry land area, his repertoire of dives was getting more and more complex. At just 13, he was performing some of the most difficult dives in the world. Andy and Sam watched in amazement as Tom scored five perfect tens at the Amateur Swimming Association National Championships – one more than Pete Waterfield, the British number one. Tom had scored enough points to qualify for the Commonwealth Games.

'He's not old enough to compete,' said Sam to Andy. 'But he'll definitely be ready for London 2012.'

'Maybe even Beijing?' Andy grinned.

Sam raised an eyebrow. The Beijing Olympics were coming up in 2008. Tom would be just 14.

Surely he was too young?

'If he carries on progressing like this, he'll qualify,' said Andy. 'Everyone's talking about 2012, but Tom has the potential to become an Olympian sooner than that. Mark my words.'

CHAPTER 11

GROWTH SPURT

'Arrrrggggghhhh!' Tom's howl of pain echoed around the pool before being muffled by the water as his head sank below the surface.

Andy jumped from his poolside seat. Tom hadn't landed flat since his very first months learning to dive – and never from the 10-metre platform. What was going on?

Under the water, Tom scrunched his eyes tight shut. Every inch of his skin stung as if he'd been burned. For a moment, he felt light-headed, before pain coursed through his body again.

'Tom?' Said Andy. 'What happened?'

Tom mustered all his strength and hauled himself out of the water, his eyes smarting with tears. He slumped onto the poolside. 'I – I don't know. Everything felt wrong. It was like I couldn't remember what to do.'

Andy's brow furrowed in sympathy. 'Do you want to try again?'

Tom shook his head. The idea of going back up to the 10-metre platform made his stomach twist with anxiety. He felt all floppy, like a rag doll – and sore where his body had hit the water with such force.

'Let's call it a night, Tom,' Andy said gently. 'Get some rest and put plenty of cream on those bruises. I'll see you tomorrow, okay?'

Tom nodded gloomily. Perhaps tomorrow would bring a new perspective.

But when he woke the next morning, his whole body ached. When his dad prepared breakfast, he couldn't eat. Not even Rob's jokes in the car on the way to school could lift his gloom. He was dreading the thought of diving practice later.

'It was just a blip, Tom,' Rob tried to reassure him. 'Everyone has bad days.'

Tom gave a small smile. He hoped his dad was right.

Later that afternoon, after school, Tom was back at Central Park Pool. He decided to dive from the 5-metre platform rather than the 10-metre one. The 10-metre board made him shudder. Five metres felt safe and friendly. As he climbed the steps, he began to feel cheerful again. Like Rob had said, last night was a blip. What had he been so nervous about? Everything was going to be fine!

He stepped to the end of the board and cleared his thoughts, preparing himself for the dive: one-and-a-half twists.

One, two, three... Jump!

But as he tumbled through the air, suddenly it wasn't fine. He was spinning too fast. Before he knew it, he had done two-and-a-half twists. Where had that extra twist come from? A wave of panic swept through him. Where was the water? Was he about to fall? All the control he had over his movements was gone, leaving him helpless in mid-air before—

'Yeeooooowwwww!' Tom felt the pain of landing before he even realised he had reached the water. The skin on his back took the impact as he slammed onto the surface. A huge splash shot up into the air, a million fast-moving droplets stinging him on every side.

His legs feeling heavy like lead, Tom kicked back to the surface then swum slowly to the edge of the pool. He hadn't got the energy to climb out. 'What's wrong with me?' he said, looking up at Andy.

Andy reached out a hand to pull him out of the water. 'It's your confidence. Last night threw you, that's all. Have another go.'

Tom nodded. He shook the water from his hair and made his way to the steps up to the board. But there was a buzzing in his ears and unwanted thoughts were crowding into his head, clamouring to make themselves heard. He tried to clear his mind, but the cacophony of worries and nerves just grew louder, a jumbled whirl of confusion, till his body began to shake. His foot was on the first step, but he couldn't go any further. It felt like he was frozen to the spot, trembling with fear.

In an instant, Andy was by his side. 'It's okay. It's okay, Tom, you don't have to do it.'

'I don't know what's going on.' Even Tom's voice was shaking. 'I'm freaking out.'

Andy could see Tom was panicking. Making him do the dive right now, he realised, would be the worst thing possible. 'Come away from the board, Tom,' he said. 'Sit down. Deep breaths. That's right.'

Once he could see that Tom was calmer, he asked, 'Can you tell me what's wrong?'

'It's like I've lost my inner compass,' Tom said. 'When I'm in the air, I can't feel where I am, like I could before. My body feels different.'

Andy frowned. Tom was 13 now. His body was

changing. 'You're growing fast at the moment,' he said. 'Your centre of gravity is changing. Your arms are longer. Your legs are longer. Your mind hasn't adjusted to the differences yet.'

Tears rolled down Tom's cheeks. He had worked so hard! It didn't seem fair that he everything was going wrong, just because his stupid body was growing.

'Hang on in there, Tom. You can do this.' Andy smiled. 'I believe in you.'

Over the next few weeks, Tom needed all his courage and determination to get from the car to the pool and then up onto the diving board. He fought his fears and tried to stay calm as his body made all its own, confusing changes. He hit his feet on the platform while turning a piked somersault. He bashed his head on the side of the pool. Bad landings caused him to smack painfully into the water. He had bruises everywhere!

But the biggest setback came at the Aachen

Junior International in Germany. The previous year, Tom had won silver at the competition. This year, having completed two dives, he had frozen on the way up the steps to perform his third dive. He panicked, just as he had back at Central Park Pool – except this time, a whole crowd was watching.

The announcer had just called his name: *'Representing Great Britain, Thomas Daley...'*

With the eyes of the crowd upon him, Tom had had to walk back down the steps and over to the recorder's desk. Trying to speak as confidently as he could, he explained that he couldn't dive.

'Thomas Daley has pulled out of the competition.' As the announcement came over the loudspeaker, Tom wished the ground would swallow him up.

'Are you sure you don't want to try the dive?' Rob asked him, as Tom joined his family up in the stands.

But this wasn't like in the early days, when Tom would change his mind while sitting in the car. He shook his head. 'I just want to go home.'

'Don't worry, there will be plenty more competitions,' Rob said, hugging him. 'Plenty more opportunities.'

But would there? Tom no longer trusted his body. When he thought about diving, he could only think of floundering in mid-air. He could only remember the horrible, sickening feeling of panic.

Right now, he felt sure he never wanted to dive again.

CHAPTER 12

REBUILDING

Luckily for Tom, there were a whole lot of people who believed in him. There were his parents, his grandparents, Andy and Sam, his teammates, Kim White and the whole team at British Swimming. There was also the sports psychologist, Michele Miller, who suggested to that Tom that he might be suffering from Lost Movement Syndrome.

'It's something gymnasts often experience,' she explained. 'They spin and flip and twist in the air like you do.'

'But why is it happening?' Tom frowned.

'Think about how complicated your dive is, Tom.

Think of all those tiny instructions your brain has to send to all the different parts of your body...'

Tom nodded. From his head to his toes, every bit of his body did something important when he dived.

'Well,' Michele continued, 'when you're tired and stressed, your brain can find it difficult to prepare for complex activities. The messages it sends to your body become confused. That's when you panic, and it feels like you've lost control.'

That makes sense, thought Tom.

'And when we panic, our instinct is to avoid danger, right?'

Tom nodded. 'So that's why I freeze and can't dive?'

'Yes. The bit of your brain that says 'diving is dangerous' starts shouting really loud, louder than the bit that's trying to tell you it's okay.'

'So what can I do?' Tom looked worried. 'Can I fix it?'

Michele smiled. 'Of course. But it means going

back to the start, teaching your brain and body to have confidence in each other. You'll need to relearn the simplest dives and build back up to the difficult ones.'

'I'll be doing really basic dives?' Tom frowned. 'I haven't done those for years.'

'It's going to take a lot of patience, Tom,' Michele said gently. 'But it's the only way.'

Tom was so frustrated to be doing basic dives again, the same dives that he had performed when he was eight. While he was practising simple jumps, tucks and pikes off the one-metre springboard, his teammate, Tonia, was performing twists and somersaults and inward dives, swooping gracefully through the air from the 10-metre platform. But Tom was glad he wasn't up there. The thought of standing at the end of the 10-metre board still sent shivers down his spine.

As the weeks went by, Tom moved from the one-metre board to three metres. Gradually Andy added somersaults, then twists. Tom started performing reverse and inward dives, and armstands too. And it seemed to be working: slowly but surely, month after month, Tom felt his confidence returning.

Then, at the end of that year, Tom finally found himself climbing the steps up to the 10-metre board. He didn't panic. He didn't freeze. He cleared his mind – and felt that familiar sense of exhilaration as he jumped from the end of the board and whooshed through the air into the clear blue water below.

Andy was relieved to see the sparkle back in Tom's eyes. He knew Tom was ready to be pushed again. It had taken almost nine months to rebuild his confidence, but Andy knew it was worth it. Tom was a once-in-a-generation diver. A truly special talent. His potential, now that he had mastered his fears, was limitless...

CHAPTER 13

SHEFFIELD

Tom stood on the edge of the ten-metre platform at the Ponds Forge pool in Sheffield. Below him, the blue tiles at the bottom of the pool gave it a dark, mysterious colour, like a deep ocean lagoon. Above him, the domed roof felt close enough to touch. As always, when he stood up here on the top platform, Tom's senses were heightened. Every echoey splash or distant shriek seemed to boom in his ears. Even the smell of the chlorine from the pool seemed sharper up here.

And today, Tom wasn't alone. Beside him was Callum Johnstone, a teenage diver from Yorkshire.

In addition to competing in individual events, most divers, including Tom, also competed in synchronised events, where they dived alongside a partner. The aim was to perform their dives perfectly in 'synch': jumping, spinning and twisting at exactly the same time.

'Ready?' asked Callum quietly.

'Yes,' Tom answered.

The two boys raised themselves onto their tiptoes, and Callum counted, 'One, two, three... go!'

They launched themselves off the board and into the air. Neither looked at the other, focusing entirely on their own dives. Together they flipped into their first somersault, then their second. Then, snapping neatly out of their tucks, they plummeted side by side into the pool.

Loud applause echoed around the auditorium. Hauling themselves out of the water, the boys grinned at each other. Each knew they had dived well. But had they been in synch?

Since he had started synchronised diving, Tom

had had to learn about a whole new scoring system. For synchro dives there were two sets of judges and two sets of scores: one for how good each dive was, and another for the synchronisation – how closely the divers mirrored each other. From the side, the two divers were supposed to look like one person. Points were lost if they landed at different angles, or spun at different speeds, or came out of their somersaults at different times.

The scores flashed up onto the board. The boys flung their arms around each other. Not only had they had performed brilliant individual dives, but they had been almost perfectly in synch!

'We did it!' whooped Tom.

Callum ruffled his younger partner's hair. 'Well done, Daley!'

The Senior National Championships here in Sheffield was the first competition at which Tom and Callum were diving together as a pair. Callum trained in Leeds, so they weren't able to train together. Their coaches were excited about the pairing. Being younger, Tom was a foot shorter than Callum, but it didn't seem to matter. They flipped and turned and fell at the same speed.

The two boys waited as the rest of the pairs completed their dives. Most were much older than Tom and Callum. At last the final pair, who were older teenagers, dived. As they uncurled from their somersaults and plunged into the water, one of them fell vertically downwards, straight as an arrow, while the other was bent slightly over, entering the water with a big splash.

'He's gone over,' said Callum. 'That's good!'

Tom was sorry for the diver who had made the error. It felt so much worse to make a mistake when you were diving with someone else. Even if they didn't say so, you knew the other person must be feeling frustrated! So far, he and Callum had both dived really well, but he wondered what Callum would say if—

'Tom!' A yelp from Callum interrupted his thoughts and suddenly he felt himself being lifted off his feet and spun around. 'We've done it!'

Tom's eyes flew to the scoreboard. At the top: Thomas Daley and Callum Johnstone. Gold medallists! They had won!

Sam and Andy hurried over, along with Callum's coach, Adrian.

'A spectacular achievement, boys,' said Andy. 'You deserve those medals!'

There were hugs all round – followed by more hugs as the two boys' families appeared poolside to congratulate them.

'How did you keep in time with each other?' asked Ben. 'It was like watching the same person twice!'

'Luck, I guess!' said Tom. And it was. Once they left the board, the boys couldn't tell what the other was doing. They just had to hope that they were in sync!

'We do slightly easier dives in the synchro than we do in the individual event,' added Callum.

'Well, something's working,' Rob grinned. 'Keep

it up, boys!'

Tom smiled. It felt special diving with someone else. It was fun to have someone to share victory with. But he knew that, later in the day, when the men's individual 10-metre competition began, he and Callum would be rivals, diving against each other!

Unfortunately for Callum, he couldn't repeat the success he had enjoyed in the synchro competition. But Tom was on fire. He blazed through the prelims, the semis, and into the final, where, for a second time, he dived to victory, cheered on by his family, coaches – and Callum.

Tom felt a glow of pride as he stepped onto the podium again. Two national golds! It hardly seemed real!

'How does it feel to be national champion?' asked Callum.

'Epic!' Tom grinned. It really did.

'I'm proud of you, mate,' smiled his partner. 'I

just want to be as good as you are!'

As the day ended, Callum went back to Leeds. Meanwhile Tom and his family set off home to Plymouth, where Tom's collection of medals, dangling like wind chimes from the ceiling, was growing month by month.

But the most exciting development of Tom's diving career was still to come...

CHAPTER 14

WORLD SERIES

'You've been invited to take part in the World Series in September!' Andy could barely contain his delight. 'You know what this means, don't you, Tom?'

Tom's eyes lit up. Of course he did! The FINA World Series was the most prestigious diving competition after the Olympic Games and the World Championships. The very best divers in the world would be competing there – including Olympic medallists!

Andy grinned. 'There will be lots of familiar faces. Callum is on the team too, and Tonia.'

The smile on Tom's face broadened. Tonia Couch was a member of the Plymouth Diving Club and one of Tom's best friends.

Tom didn't have to go far for his first World Series competition. The event was being held in Sheffield, where he had triumphed earlier that same year, 2007. As well as competing in the individual event, Tom would also be diving with Callum in the men's synchro.

As usual, it was the synchro event that was held first. But this time the competitors were in a different league. Tom and Callum watched in awe as the talented international divers landed one stunning dive after another. The Chinese divers were especially impressive.

'How will we ever beat them?' whispered Tom.

Callum shrugged. 'I don't think we will. Not this time!'

Neither Tom nor Callum spoke as they climbed the steps to the platform for their final dive. But they could sense each other's nerves. At the top, they gave each other a good-luck fist bump.

The boys were already in synch as they walked to the end of the platform and settled themselves on the edge. Tom breathed deeply and tried to calm his pounding heart. As Callum began the count, he flexed his legs and raised himself onto the tips of his toes.

'One, two, three... go!'

Below on the poolside, their teammates, including Tonia, held their breath as they watched Tom and Callum spin at lightning speed through the air before swooping down into the water, making two small, synchronised splashes.

Applause rang out as the scores appeared. 388.89 points. Tom and Callum looked at each other and grinned. It wouldn't win them a medal, but they could be extremely proud of this effort.

'Where do you think we'll come?' asked Callum.

Tom grinned. 'Isn't that tempting fate? I'm going to say sixth.'

'Fifth.' Callum replied. 'I bet you.'

When all the divers had finished and the final scores were in, Callum's optimism was rewarded. The boys had finished in fifth position.

'Congratulations!' Tonia hugged them both. 'That's a pretty amazing result against that lot!'

In fact, the whole GB team was buzzing. Tonia had made it to the final of the women's platform competition. Ben Swain had made it to the final of the men's three-metre springboard. Tandi Gerrard and Rebecca Gallantree had finished fourth in the women's three-metre synchro final.

'How are you feeling about tomorrow, Tom?' asked Tonia. The men's individual event would be held the next day.

Tom grinned. 'I can't wait.'

It was true. Now that he had competed once against these incredible international divers, he wasn't scared anymore. 'Bring it on!'

Tom finished second in his semi-final group, behind the world championship silver medallist Zhou Lüxin.

'Not too shabby, Daley,' Callum grinned.

He was right. Zhou Lüxin was a formidable competitor. But even more formidable was his Chinese teammate, Lin Yue, whom Tom would also face in the final.

In the end, the two Chinese divers took gold and silver with ease. Behind them the Russian Gleb Galperin, the reigning world champion, took bronze. But to everyone's amazement, just five points behind Gleb was...

Thomas Daley!

Tom's 467.45 points had been enough to put him in fourth place. It was an epic achievement. At just 13, Tom was holding his own against the strongest divers on the planet!

And Andy knew Tom had more to offer. He knew Tom was capable of bigger, more complicated dives. He didn't want to overwhelm young Tom, whose confidence had been at rock bottom not so long ago. But now was the time to think ambitiously. And Andy's ambition for Tom was big...

International medals.

Bronze. Silver. Perhaps even gold.

CHAPTER 15

AMBITION

Peter Waterfield

Blake Aldridge

Ben Swain

Hayley Sage

Tandi Gerrard

Nick Robinson-Baker

Stacie Powell

Rebecca Gallantree

Tonia Couch

Thomas Daley

It was official. The GB diving team for Beijing 2008

had been announced and Tom was on it!

A year of hard work had led up to this moment. With an ambitious programme of new dives, Tom had won gold at the 2007 British Championships. He had also triumphed in the synchro event, where he had been paired with an older diver, Blake Aldridge.

Two weeks later, he had missed school to travel to Spain for the prestigious Madrid Grand Prix, where he had won bronze in the individual competition and silver with Blake in the synchro event.

At the World Cup in Beijing, Tom and Blake had won bronze in the synchro competition and set a new British record. It had been Tom's biggest, most important competition so far, and he had been its youngest ever male medallist.

Then in March 2008, he had won gold at the European Championships in the Netherlands. He was the youngest ever European champion.

Now, at 14, Tom was about to become the youngest British Olympian for over 50 years. Andy had been right. Young as he was, British Swimming could not ignore Tom's talent. Not to include him on the team would be madness.

And Tom's successes hadn't just been in the pool. He had been nominated for, and had won, the 2007 BBC Young Sports Personality of the Year award.

The whole family accompanied Tom to the red carpet event at the BBC Studios in London. It was so glamorous! Everyone was dressed up and on their very best behaviour. Well, mostly...

'Tom!' Will hissed. 'You have to see this! Look!'

Tom spun round. 'What's going on?'

Will nodded his head in Rob's direction.

Tom gasped. 'He isn't!'

Will pulled a face. 'He is!'

Rob, the prankster, was drinking his beer out of Tom's glass trophy!

'I guess I'm never going to get big-headed,' grinned Tom. 'Not with Dad around.'

But, deep down, he knew he had the proudest dad in the world.

As Tom's fame grew, his packed schedule kept the whole family busy. Rob liked to call himself Tom's taxi driver. The green metallic van with its famous Dixie horn was always on the road, ferrying Tom from training to school, then to competitions and his other commitments... which were becoming more and more varied. Tom had been offered a modelling deal with Adidas. Will loved to tease him about that! He was invited to become the patron of several charities. Celebrities wanted to meet him. He was doing interviews for TV, radio and magazines... all while training six hours a day, six days a week... *and* going to school!

Organising Tom's schedule was Debs' job. 'I guess that makes me your PA,' she joked. 'I could do with a payrise, Tom. Especially with the Olympics coming up.'

Tom's family would be travelling with him to Beijing, though British Swimming regulations prevented them from staying in the same hotel. But by now, Tom was used to travelling the world to compete. New rooms, new food, new faces. He took it all in his stride.

'Don't forget your lucky monkey, Tom,' said Rob. 'You haven't packed him.'

'Dad! I'm too old!' he groaned. 'What if Blake sees him?' Tom would be sharing a room with his synchro partner, Blake, who was twelve years older. Tom was sure *he* didn't travel with a lucky mascot.

Rob pulled a sad face but Tom was firm. No lucky monkey, not this time.

But when Tom's back was turned, Rob slipped the lucky monkey into his bag, under the Team GB kit. What if Tom missed home? What if it really was lucky?

Best to be on the safe side, thought Rob with a smile. *You just never know.*

CHAPTER 16

BEIJING

Standing in the centre of Beijing, 14-year-old Tom had never felt so small. This city was bigger, brighter, busier than anywhere he had ever been before. He craned his neck towards the sky, marvelling at the skyscrapers that reached up on all sides of him. Monuments, cinemas, shops, restaurants... everything was huge here. And there were so many people! They seemed to be oblivious to the hubbub of noise: honking cars and buses, the shouts of street food sellers, a cacophony of bicycle bells, the loud blasts of music from shops and cafés.

Tom and his teammates also had to acclimatise to

the humidity of China's capital city. It was August and the temperature was a sweltering 38 degrees Celsius, with the air full of moisture. It was like being in a giant steam room!

In addition to the sights of the city, and the amazing Great Wall of China beyond it, Tom, Tonia and their teammates had the whole of the Olympic Village to explore. Once again, everything was so big! There were towering accommodation blocks, cinemas, shops, even a hair salon. Most exciting of all was the vast dining hall, built to accommodate thousands of athletes at a time.

'It's open 24 hours a day!' cried Tom.

'And it's free!' added Tonia.

There were different sections where you could eat food from all over the world, from China to India to the Caribbean...

'Or McDonald's,' laughed Tom.

'We're going to do that, I guarantee,' she smiled. 'Wait, Tom. Is that..?'

Tom spun round to where she was pointing

and let out a yelp of surprise. It was the Jamaican sprinter, Usain Bolt, the fastest man on the planet!

'Shall we go and say hi?' suggested Tom, then laughed as he saw Tonia's face. 'Joking! Of course we're not going to say hi. He's, like... *Usain Bolt!*'

But Usain Bolt wasn't the only celebrity in the village. Diving was a massive sport in China, and Tom was surprised to find that lots of the Chinese staff, along with many of the Chinese athletes, recognised him. As a diver *and* the youngest competitor at the Games, it seemed Tom was already famous here in Beijing! His Chinese fans even had nicknames for him: Baby Daley, Little Briton, Peking Tom... Tom turned bright red the first time someone called out to him – 'Baby Daley!' – and asked for his autograph. But he soon got used to it.

'You're loving this, aren't you!' teased Tonia.

Tom grinned. He couldn't deny it. It was fun to be recognised!

The number eight is considered lucky in Chinese culture, so the opening ceremony of the Games was held at 8.00 pm on 8 August 2008. Tom, Tonia, Ben Swain and their new friends, the tennis players Andy and Jamie Murray, passed the time before the athletes' parade by playing cards. The holding area deep inside the stadium was hot and humid. Tom's GB suit had looked smart when he put it on, but after a couple of hours waiting in the sweltering heat, it looked like he'd been swimming in it!

But the heat and the long, tedious wait were soon forgotten when the time came to walk out into the famous Beijing National Stadium, known as the Bird's Nest. As Tom emerged from the tunnel into the arena, clutching his Union Jack flag, he was hit by an extraordinary blast of noise and colour. Some 80,000 spectators packed the stands, cheering and waving the flags of every nation. The arena captured the noise like a huge bowl, amplifying it into a giant wall of sound. On the pitch were drummers with neon drumsticks, whirling dancers with in red and gold costumes that looked like flames, and the sky was lit up by the biggest, most spectacular fireworks display that Tom had ever seen.

But the most dramatic moment of all came as the Olympic torch entered the stadium, carried by Ning Li, a famous Chinese gymnast. The arena plunged suddenly into darkness, and, as if by magic, Ning was lifted into the air and sent flying around the edge of the stadium, the burning torch held high. At the end of the lap, he touched the flame to the side of the arena, setting it alight. Tom gasped as a wall of fire travelled around the stadium towards a vast cauldron towering above the roof. As the fire reached it, the cauldron burst into flame, a blaze of burning gold that lit up the entire arena.

All around Tom, the athletes watched with amazement. None of them had seen a spectacle like this. Then the cheers erupted. A huge grin of pride and excitement spread across Tom's face. Around him were the best athletes in the world: runners, rowers, cyclists, boxers, equestrians, weightlifters, high-jumpers... And here he was. He was part of it. Part of this incredible celebration of sport.

He couldn't wait to take his place on the 10-metre platform and represent his country!

The diving competition took place in the Olympic Aquatic Centre, known as the Water Cube. From outside, the building glowed with the colour of a tropical lagoon, a magical cube of brilliant, sparkling blue. A shiver of excitement ran down Tom's spine every time he saw it. Inside the Centre, the lights were bright and the atmosphere was buzzing. Diving was one of China's favourite sports, and the stands were packed with spectators, thousands of them, cheering on divers of every nationality.

The smile didn't leave Tom's face once. The excitement of the crowd, the camaraderie of his GB teammates, the sight of his family up in the stands. And then, the thrill of swooping through the air in the middle of this incredible venue... It felt to Tom like he was in a dream.

Tom's list was challenging, but the support from the crowd felt incredible. He dived the best he ever had – tumbling and twisting through the prelims, soaring through the semis, and making it to the finals, where he finished in seventh place.

'You did it!' Rob flung his arms around his son. 'You can be very, very proud of yourself, Tom.'

'Well done, my love.' Debs piled in, followed by Will and Ben. Tom found himself at the centre of a Daley family huddle.

'Ugh! Soggy!' joked Will.

Tom grinned. He hadn't won. He hadn't expected to. But he felt a glow of pride and happiness. He had dived his way to the Olympic final! And having his family here, supporting him, was the best feeling of all.

'I'm impressed, Tom – 463.55 points,' added Andy. From the preliminary round, through the semi-final to the final, Tom's scores had gone up and up. 'You handled the pressure brilliantly.'

Will was busy scrolling on his phone. 'Apparently

1.3 billion people watched you dive on TV.'

Tom's eyes were wide. 'Wow! That's incredible,' he said, though he felt a bit relieved he hadn't known that while he was up on the platform. Talk about pressure!

Tom was sad to leave Beijing. He would miss hanging out with his GB teammates. He would miss the Olympic Village and spotting the world's most famous athletes. He would miss the magical atmosphere of the Water Cube where the diving competition had taken place. He would miss feeling part of something really special, a celebration that brought the whole world together.

Life would feel very normal back in Plymouth...

CHAPTER 17

A NEW CHAPTER

Tom took a deep breath and bowed slightly. Speak clearly, he reminded himself. And smile!

'Your Royal Highness,' he said.

The Queen reached out a white-gloved hand and Tom took it. Phew! He had remembered the instruction: don't offer your hand till the Queen holds out hers!

'Very well done,' said Her Majesty, with a small smile, before moving down the line to the next person.

Tom let out a breath. Nothing had gone wrong. Thank goodness! He wondered what would happen if something *did* go wrong? What if you said the wrong thing? Used the wrong name? Accidentally burped or something? Would you be carried off in disgrace by a footman?!

Tom turned to watch as his fellow GB teammates greeted Her Majesty. Everyone was dressed in their smartest outfits. The men bowed slightly and the women gave a small curtsey as the Queen passed down the line. There were nervous smiles on everyone's faces. It wasn't every day they were invited to a reception in the glittering ballroom at Buckingham Palace!

As a waiter in a tailcoat passed by and held out a silver platter containing delicious-looking food, Tom had a funny feeling that life wasn't going to return to normal any time soon.

He was right. In the weeks that followed, Tom's life only got crazier. He met Tiger Woods, Dizzee Rascal, the cast of the Harry Potter films, Nick Grimshaw, Geri Halliwell and Gary Lineker... The list went on and on. It seemed 14-year-old Tom Daley had become an A-lister!

Tom went to the Pride of Britain Awards, and took part in the Royal Variety Performance, alongside Leona Lewis, Take That and Rihanna. He joined the athletes' bus parade around central London. And with Tonia, he switched on the Plymouth Christmas lights.

He even did a photoshoot swimming with sharks at the National Marine Aquarium in Plymouth. The three sharks, named Emily, Enzo and Howardine, were held at a distance by their trainers using long sticks, while the photographer directed Tom to press his hands against the glass of the tank. He'd never been more scared in his life!

Life after the Olympics had turned out be full on, and Tom was glad to be back at training at Central Park Pool. It was the normality he needed.

But school was a different matter...

It was Monday morning. Tom slowed down as he

approached the school gates. His heart felt heavier with every step. How long would it be before someone tried to trip him up? How long would it be before someone threw something? Or started calling him names?

'Oi! Speedo Boy!'

Thirty seconds exactly. Tom picked up his pace. He knew what was coming next. If only he could get into the building, into the eyesight of a teacher before—

Too late. Tom was cornered. A group of older kids surrounded him.

'We're coming for you at lunchtime, Speedo Boy.'

'Don't try to hide.'

'Think you're better than us, don't you?'

Tom gulped.

'Well?' growled the bullies.

Tom felt sweat beading on his forehead. *Don't say anything. It'll only make it worse.*

Just in time the bell rang. A teacher was heading towards them and the group dispersed. Tom felt a surge of relief, quickly followed by anger. It wasn't fair! It wasn't his fault he'd been to the Olympics! It wasn't his fault he'd won medals and been on TV. Rob said the kids were just jealous. But that didn't make it any easier.

He felt sick as he plodded towards his classroom. Thank goodness for his friends, Harriet, Sophie, Nikita and Alex. He knew they would stand up for him whenever they could. But still, Tom wished he could be anywhere else than here.

And the day had barely begun...

In class, someone threw a pair of scissors at his head.

Someone else emptied his pencil case all over the floor.

At lunchtime, he was rugby tackled to the ground – again. This time, it had really hurt. Tom landed on his wrists. By the time the bell rang for home time, they had swollen to double their normal size.

As usual, Rob was waiting in the car to take him to Central Park Pool. His face fell as Tom held out his hands. 'Look at what they did!' There were tears in Tom's eyes. 'I can't go back, Dad. I can't do it. Please!'

'What happened, Tom?'

Tom told his dad everything. Rob knew Tom had been struggling with bullies, but he was shocked that it had got this bad. With swollen wrists, Tom couldn't dive for five days – and Rob and Debs agreed: Tom wouldn't be going back to Eggbuckland Community College.

A huge weight lifted from Tom's shoulders. But that left the problem of where he would go to school to finish his GCSEs, and where he would study for his A-levels.

The Daleys needn't have worried. Tom was immediately offered a scholarship at Plymouth College. He loved his new school immediately. The grey brick buildings with their fancy turrets and lattice windows reminded him of Hogwarts. His new teachers created a special timetable, scheduled around his training. And lots of his classmates did elite sports. Here he didn't feel different. The only rugby tackling here was during sports matches!

Rob and Debs breathed a huge sigh of relief. Tom was smiling again.

CHAPTER 18

ROME

Rob Daley sat high up in the stands at Foro Italico, Rome's Olympic pool. Below, the blue water sparkled invitingly in the sunshine. Beyond the stadium, lofty pine trees dotted the horizon. There was a broad smile on Rob's face as he held his giant Union Jack above his head. He loved to be outdoors, and he knew Tom did too. His son was always at his happiest when he was diving under a clear summer sky.

And there he was – Tom had just appeared at the back the 10-metre platform. Rob gave a supportive cheer and waved his flag. He hoped Tom could hear him, and know he was willing him on, every step, jump, flip and twist of the way!

Tom had finished fifth in the prelims and third in the semi-finals. So far, so good. But Rob knew Tom was worried: his list of dives had a lower tariff than any of his competitors. In order to win a medal, he would have to dive them all perfectly.

Rob cheered as Tom performed a stunning first dive. The judges gave it a succession of 8s. *Keep it up, son!* thought Rob. *You can do this!*

Dive two. A forward three-and-a-half somersaults. From the back of the platform, Tom launched into his hurdle steps – a bit like skipping, Rob always thought – before hurling himself off the board and becoming a tight whirling ball spinning through the air. In the blink of an eye, it was over. There was barely a splash as Tom hit the water. 'Well done!' shouted Rob.

The judges scored him 81.00, which included a couple of 9s. But it wasn't a particularly difficult dive. With a tariff of just 3.00, it was the easiest dive in Tom's programme.

Dive three. An inward three-and-a-half tuck. Tariff 3.2. As Tom teetered on the end of the board with his back to the water, Rob's heart beat a little faster. What if he toppled?

But Tom didn't topple. Tom's dive was neat and precise, and awarded him 89.4 points – more 9s! Tom was in fourth place now, just one point behind the medals, and Rob's grin broadened.

Dive four. Armstand back triple somersault tuck. Rob was always amazed by his son's strength and control as he rose up into the armstand balance. It was crazy, when he thought about it – his son was standing upside down on a platform 10 metres up in the air, in the middle of Rome! Rob gripped his flag tightly with both hands as Tom launched himself into the air.

Oh, yes! Rob knew a brilliant dive when he saw one. From way up in the sky, Tom flew effortlessly through the air and slid perfectly into the water. He scored 86.4 points. Brilliant!

Dive five. Back three-and-a-half somersaults. Tom's favourite dive. Rob knew his son would give it everything he had. *Come on, Tom!*

Yes: 97.35! Four 10s! Rob squealed with delight. From fourth place, Tom had moved up into third!

It was time for the final dive, dive six. Reverse three-and-a-half somersaults. A tariff of 3.4. Rob clenched his fists nervously. The other divers had saved their hardest dives for last. All except Tom. To make up for the easier dive, Tom would need to perform it to perfection. Rob's heart went out to Tom, standing at the edge of the board. *Make it good. No, make it great!*

Facing the pool, Tom leapt up and forward before arching backwards into the somersault, his head sweeping perilously close to the concrete platform. Rob winced. He hated to watch the reverse dives – they were so dangerous! Tom spun like a Catherine wheel, before dropping towards the pool to the sound of wild applause. It was good, Rob knew that. But was it perfect? *Please let it be perfect!*

Four 10s! Now Tom was guaranteed a medal. Rob blinked. His son would be a world championship medallist! But which colour would the medal be? It was too soon to tell. There were still two divers left...

Rob held his breath as he watched the Australian diver in first place land awkwardly, tipping backwards, losing points. Then the Chinese diver landed in the pool at a sideways angle. He too lost points. Rob's heart was thumping in his chest. *Could it... Was it...?*

Yes! There, in majestic glowing digits, was the result: Thomas Daley, 539.85 points. Tom was the gold medal winner!

Rob's eyes darted from the scoreboard to the poolside, seeking out his son. Tom's hands were covering his face in disbelief. But when he took them away, Rob could see his grin of delight. It took every ounce of his strength not to run down from the stands to give his son a massive bear hug. *Wait*, he told himself. *Tom has to collect his medal first!*

And he did. Rob watched, brimming with pride, as his teenage son stepped onto the podium, his gold medal glinting in the early evening sun. Was it possible? His little boy was the world champion? The same little boy he'd taken to his first diving lesson aged eight. Rob flung his arms into the air for joy, while cheers of delight and enthusiasm rang around the pool.

As the crowd of journalists and officials around the podium began to disperse, Rob hurried from his seat to the poolside. Time to congratulate Tom! Time for that long-awaited hug!

But Tom had gone.

Rob spotted a throng of people disappearing into the building. Waving his visitor pass in a confident sort of way, Rob followed the group and found himself at the back of the press conference. Tom and Andy were sitting at a desk at the front, facing a large huddle of journalists and camera crew, calling out questions for the new world champion. Without hesitation, Rob piped up: 'I'd like to ask a question.'

'Which publication are you from?' asked the compere.

'I'm Tom's dad. Tom, can you give me a cuddle?' Rob knew Tom would be embarrassed and sure enough Tom's face went pillar-box red. But he didn't care. 'Come on, Tom. Please!'

Smiling sheepishly, the world champion left his seat and shuffled through the crowd. Rob flung his arms around his son, weeping tears of joy.

To their surprise, the crowd of journalists erupted into loud applause.

'I'm so proud of you, Tom,' Rob said. 'You can't imagine how proud I am!'

But Tom could. Only his loyal, loud, silly, amazing dad would be proud enough to sneak into a press conference... for a hug!

CHAPTER 19

TRAGEDY

Tom was back home. He was back in training. He was back at school, studying for his GCSEs. And, aged just 15, he was the British, European and *World* Champion, the first diver ever to hold all three titles at once. There would be a lot of pressure on Tom during the year ahead.

'2010 is going to be a tough one, Tom,' warned Andy. 'It's hard being out in front. Everybody else is chasing you, hungry to beat you.'

'I understand.' Tom nodded. Right now, though, it didn't feel like anything could burst his bubble. He felt on top of the world.

So far, Tom had risen to every challenge. But would he be tough enough to survive this kind of pressure?

The first title that Tom would have to defend was that of British Champion. All Tom's family – his parents, his brother, and his four grandparents – would be travelling to Sheffield to support him. He and Andy had been working on a new dive: a back two-and-a-half somersaults, two-and-a-half twists with a tariff of 3.6. It was a scary dive and every time Tom attempted it, his stomach churned with fear. But if everything went to plan, this big dive would earn him big points.

There was a problem, though. Tom had injured his shoulder in training. He had never been injured before, not really. Now, pain gnawed at him constantly. It distracted and frustrated him. It made him scared of hurting himself again – and it made him extra-scared of attempting his new twisting dive.

Tom qualified for the final easily, but here he found himself dropping behind his more experienced GB teammate, Pete Waterfield. All his determination and focus weren't enough to claw his way to the top of the leaderboard.

For the first time in four years, Tom had lost his title. He was no longer the British champion.

'Onwards and upwards,' Rob told him. 'You can win it back next year, Tom.'

'Focus on the European Championships,' said Andy.

Tom was disappointed but he gritted his teeth, determined to push himself even harder by learning another challenging dive: the front four-and-a-half somersaults with tuck, tariff 3.7. To help Tom master it, Andy arranged for a special rig to be fitted above the pool. Buckled into the harness, Tom spun and tucked above the pool, before plunging into the water and being pulled out on a rope by Andy.

In August, a few months after Tom had sat his GCSE exams, Rob travelled with him to Budapest for the European Championships. But there was more disappointment to face. While practising the troublesome twisting dive, Tom pulled a muscle in his arm. He was in too much pain to continue. The disappointment of not being able to compete was a huge blow.

And this new injury it was far from being the only thing on Tom's mind...

Four years earlier, in 2006, Rob had been diagnosed with a brain tumour. He had had an operation, along with chemotherapy, but the cancer had come back. While Tom travelled from Budapest to Singapore for the Youth Olympics, Rob returned home to start a new course of chemo. It was the first time that Tom had travelled to a competition without his dad. Tom hoped and prayed that, like last time, Rob's treatment would be successful. It would be months before they would know the outcome.

While Rob underwent treatment back in Plymouth, in Singapore, an MRI scan of Tom's arm revealed a bad tear to his tricep. Once again, Tom had no choice but to pull out of the competition. Another blow. It seemed as though Andy was right:

2010 was shaping up to be the toughest year yet.

Tom summoned all his positivity. Even though he wouldn't be competing, he travelled with the rest of the team to Tucson, USA, for the Junior World Championships. It was so frustrating not being able to compete, but he did his best to cheer on his teammates, and support his family via FaceTime, while the physiotherapists helped him recover from his injury.

Finally, at the end of August, there was something to celebrate. Tom's GCSE results had arrived. Eight A* grades! Six hours a day of training plus competitions hadn't prevented Tom from studying hard. His teachers at Plymouth College had got used to marking his work and messaging it to him wherever he was in the world!

Despite the camaraderie of his GB teammates, Tom couldn't help wishing he was back home celebrating with his friends. He had been away for seven weeks now. He missed Plymouth and his family. He missed his mum and his brothers.

And most of all, he missed his dad, his jokes, his hugs, and seeing him in the stands with his massive Union Jack.

Finally, in September, Tom returned to Plymouth. There was just enough time to see his family, spend time with Rob and hang out with his friends before, in October, he travelled with the rest of the team to Delhi for the Commonwealth Games. Could he put in a winning performance and end the year on a high?

At home, Rob, Debs and the boys were glued to the TV. On day one of the diving, they watched as Tom and his new synchro partner, Max Brick, beat the Olympic champion, Matt Mitcham and his partner Ethan Warren, to win gold in the synchronised event.

'That's my boy!' roared Rob.

'Easy, Dad,' laughed Will. 'Doctor's orders.'

Rob had just started his second round of chemo. But it was hard to keep calm when his son had just won a Commonwealth gold!

The individual event the next day was Tom's biggest challenge so far. He would be performing his back two-and-a-half somersaults, two-and-a-half twists.

'He hates that dive,' Rob said.

It was true. Tom had come to fear and loathe the 'twister' or 'demon dive'. The complicated series of movements made him feel out of control, like a toy tumbling from a shelf. It took all his inner strength to climb the steps to the platform every time he had to perform it.

But today, diving against Matt Mitcham and his own synchro partner, Max, Tom's nerves seemed to magically vanish. As his feet left the platform, he seemed to soar though the air like a bird, defying gravity, before tumbling and twisting with the grace of a gymnast.

'That's how you do it!' whooped Rob. 'Barely a splash.'

The whole family jumped up and down on the sofa as Tom performed one spectacular dive after another. His third dive, an inward three-and-a-half somersault tuck, scored perfect 10s from all seven judges. He finished with 538.35 points to Matt's 509.15.

'I've never seen him dive better than that!' said Rob. 'He'll be on the Olympic podium next, you'll see.'

Tom was destined for glory; everyone was sure of it. But Rob, his loudest and proudest, supporter, wouldn't be there to cheer him on for much longer. The doctors declared that his brain tumour had become too big to operate on, too big for chemo to work. Just a few months later, in May 2011, Rob died, surrounded by his loving family, including Tom.

Grieving the loss of his father would take months and years. For now, Tom threw himself into training. Diving, competing, and the support of Andy and his teammates, provided the normality that he needed.

And he was, more than ever, determined to do his dad proud.

CHAPTER 20

REDIVE

After seven long years of waiting, 2012, Olympic year, had arrived. London was buzzing, packed with hundreds of thousands of athletes and fans, ready to enjoy a month of sport. All British hopes were on Jessica Ennis, Mo Farah, Tom Daley...

Tom felt an exhilarating mix of emotions. Pressure, pride, passion. He couldn't wait for the start of the diving competition. He couldn't wait to represent Great Britain at the home Olympics, the only home Games he and his teammates would experience in their lifetime.

Tom had swept easily though the prelims and the

semis. But tonight would decide everything. It was the night of the final.

Outside, dusk had fallen over the city. The summer evening was hot and heavy with expectation. Inside the Aquatics Centre, the lights were burning bright and the atmosphere was at fever pitch. Just a few hundred metres away, in the main stadium, Mo Farah had won gold for Great Britain in the 5000 metres. Now, the eyes of the country were on Tom Daley in the men's 10-metre final. The entire GB diving team was there to support him. Debs and Will were up in the stands, holding their 'Go Tom' banner high. And was that...? Yes, it was – David Beckham was sitting in the front row with his sons, Brooklyn and Romeo.

Still just eighteen, Tom wasn't the favourite to win. The competition included far more experienced divers. But would the support of a home crowd carry him into a medal-winning position?

Tom had chosen to start with one of his most difficult dives: the famous 'Twister'. Tonight, his strongest competitors, the Chinese divers Lin Yue and Qiu Bo, would be diving after him. Qiu Bo had triumphed in the World Series, earning 25 perfect 10s and a record-breaking total of 609.20 points. Competition didn't come much fiercer than this!

As he climbed the steps to the 10-metre platform, Tom felt the familiar combination of fear and excitement. He heard the short splash as the diver before him hit the water, followed by cheers from the crowd. Then, as Tom emerged onto the platform, the cheers turned into an explosion of delight and excitement.

Tom's focus was total, though. He stepped calmly to the edge of the platform, turned his back to the pool and cleared his mind of everything but the dive. With control, he reached his arms to the sky, raised himself onto tiptoes, bent his knees and leapt, arcing gracefully into the first somersault...

But something was wrong. As Tom searched frantically for a spot on the ceiling to focus on, the flash of cameras around the pool made him blink.

They glittered in his peripheral vision. Without the all-important spot to focus on, his timing coming out of his somersaults was wrong. He was falling at an angle and instead of his usual smooth entry, he sent a plume of spray upwards as he struck the water.

The home crowd cheered Tom's dive with enthusiasm, but Tom didn't hear them. As he resurfaced, every muscle in his body was clenched in frustration. There was a single thought in his mind: redive. He knew that his chance of a medal depended on being allowed to perform the dive again. Hundreds of fans were watching in the Aquatics Centre. Millions more were watching on TV. Tom was holding up the competition. But he didn't care. Without waiting to see his score, he marched over to the judging desk.

'Please, you have to let me dive again,' Tom begged. 'There were cameras flashing. There shouldn't be cameras.'

Andy joined him in support. Flash photography was strictly forbidden in the diving pool. But would the judges agree to the redive? Not even Andy could remember a time when a redive had been allowed.

Just then, Tom's score appeared on the electronic scoreboard: 75.6. Tom shook his head. He knew he would have done better if it wasn't for those spectators with their cameras, if only they knew what their photography might be costing him!

Finally, there came the nod that Tom and Andy were waiting for. They exchanged a look of relief. The announcer addressed the crowd in a firm tone: 'No flash photography.'

As he climbed the steps, Tom's heart was pounding. But this time, fear and excitement were mixed with pride. His dad had always told him not to worry about what other people might think. Well, he hadn't. He had stood up for himself and for what was fair – no matter what the crowd or the judges or his fellow competitors might think. He knew Rob would have been proud of him.

For a second time, Tom leapt from the edge of the platform into the air. This time, he spun and twisted to perfection. Less than two seconds later, he plunged into the water, gliding through the surface with a rip entry. As he resurfaced, the noise of the crowd was deafening.

His score: 91.80.

Yes! Tom grinned with relief. The redive had paid off!

At the end of the first round, Tom was in fourth position, behind the two Chinese divers, Lin and Qiu, and the American David Boudia.

Tom's second dive was a lower tariff, just 3.2. The judges scored it 86.4.

The Chinese divers both excelled, each scoring 94.05.

Dive three was another of Tom's biggest dives, an armstand back three somersaults. At 92.75, it was his highest scoring dive so far. But this time it was the American's chance to shine, taking the lead with 99.9 points. Tom was still in fourth position. Could he overtake? Would one of the others make a mistake?

Tom's hardest dive was next, with a tariff of 3.7. He whirled at top speed through the air, slicing into the pool with immaculate precision. He scored 98.05! His teammates whooped for joy. But would his stunning dive be enough to take him up the leaderboard? They would only know once David, Lin and Qiu had dived.

Lin performed a complicated dive but landed badly. David and Qiu performed brilliant dives but neither of their performances was as strong as Tom's. He had edged into third place.

The cheers for Tom were getting more intense every time he appeared on the platform. Joy and positivity resonated around the Aquatics Centre, sending him jumping higher and spinning faster.

There were just two more dives left. Tom's fifth dive was another tricky one. He propelled himself through the air with grace and once again, it was a ripped entry.

It was 97.2 – his second highest score of the night.

The tension in the auditorium was electric. As his name flashed up in first place on the leaderboard, it felt to Tom like the roof could fly off the building, blasted away by the noise of this excited home crowd. Gold medal position! He could hardly believe it.

Could he hold onto it in the final round? One thing was for sure, none of these competitors was going to give up without a fight!

Tom had saved his easiest dive for last. The tariff was just 3.3. He knew the other divers, David, Qiu and Lin, would be finishing on harder, higher-scoring dives. To achieve the score he needed, Tom's dive would have to be perfect, or as close to perfect as he could make it.

Poised on the edge of the platform, he stared down at the Olympic rings and the magical words 'London 2012' shimmering at the bottom of the pool. Every dive had been leading to this moment. Standing here was the thing he had been dreaming of all his life.

This is for you, Dad.

Seconds later, Tom pulled himself out of the water. The crowd were on their feet, and Tom felt a bubble of sheer happiness explode inside him. He had done everything he possibly could. His score: 90.75. He was so far ahead of Lin that the Chinese diver wouldn't catch him, even with perfect scores. Tom's eyes flew to his mum and Will, madly waving their 'Go, Tom!' banner. Finally the pressure was off. He could relax.

Sitting with his teammates in the stands, he clapped as David scored an epic 102.60. Lin scored a strong 90.00, and Qiu an impressive 100.08. He didn't need to look at the scoreboard to know the outcome. David had won gold, Qiu silver, and he... he had won a magnificent bronze medal!

Even if it had been gold, Tom could not have felt happier or prouder. As he stepped up to the podium to collect his medal, he waved his thanks and appreciation to the crowd, to Andy, his family, his fans. Right now, diving felt like the most wonderful thing in the world. The Aquatics Centre felt like the centre of the universe. And he, Tom Daley, was the happiest teenager on the planet.

CHAPTER 21

SPLASH!

Despite all the attention from the media following the Olympics, there definitely wasn't any risk of Tom getting too big for his boots. In the Daley household, his brothers would never let that happen.

'Ha, ha, third place!' joked Will. 'Third place, third place!'

'Let's see your Olympic medal then,' laughed Tom. 'Oh, wait...'

'Stop it, boys,' smiled Debs. 'The joke's getting old.' But secretly she was glad that her boys still squabbled as they always did. Life without Rob was tough – thank goodness her sons and their bickering never changed. 'So tell us about this TV programme you've been invited to take part in, Tom.'

'It's called *Splash!*, Mum,' Tom replied. 'On ITV. It's like *Strictly* but with diving.'

Tom's role on the show would be to mentor a group of celebrities learning to dive. Once their training was finished, he would do a synch dive with each of the finalists off the 10-metre platform.

'*Splash!?* Isn't the whole point of diving not to make a splash?' grinned Will.

'Yeah, I guess they should call the programme *Rip Entry*.'

'*Or As Little Splash As Possible,*' joked Will.

Tom pulled a face. 'They've asked Andy to take part as a judge, and Leon Taylor too.' The former Olympic diver Leon Taylor was one of Tom's biggest childhood heroes.

'You've always said you want to work in TV eventually,' said his mum.

Tom nodded. He knew what she was thinking: 'eventually' meant 'at the end of your diving career'. And she was right. Divers usually retired before they were 30. Tom was just 18. He had plenty of time left in the sport, assuming he didn't get injured. But diving wouldn't last forever. Tom loved vlogging and, later on, he had a feeling he might enjoy a career in TV.

'I'm going to say yes,' said Tom. 'It'll be good experience.'

Tom was glad to have something new to focus on. He hated to admit it, but now that the Olympics was over, he felt a little... flat. It was like the feeling he had after a dive sometimes, when all that adrenaline and buzz suddenly disappeared.

The pool at Luton Sports Village, which was transformed into a TV studio while filming took place, quickly became Tom's second home. Being part of a TV show was like being part of a big family. There were the production crew, the dive trainers, Tom's fellow presenters, Vernon Kay and Gabby Logan... and, of course, the celebrity divers.

There were plenty of belly flops as the divers started their training, lots of bruises – and a few tears too! It reminded Tom of his first few lessons at Central Park Pool. Some of the celebs were fearless. Some were scared of everything: water, heights, jumping from the platform. Tom understood. He had been there. In fact, he was *still* there, every day.

'Even I get scared on the 10-metre platform,' he told the divers.

The celebrities looked shocked. 'Really?'

Tom grinned. 'Every single time. Diving from a massive height isn't natural. You're asking your body to do something really weird and scary! But it's about facing your fears and stepping outside your comfort zone.'

It was true. Tom loved to see the celebrity divers get braver with every session. He loved to see them conquer their fears week by week. He hoped they would fall in love with diving like he had!

Over five million viewers watched the first episode of *Splash!* With glitz and glamour, the flashing lights, make-up and fancy, jewelled swimwear, it was far from the reality of training to dive. But Tom was excited about bringing diving to a whole new audience. Everyone in the country knew about running and swimming. Now it was time to put diving on the map!

And Tom's bubbly personality was perfect in front of the cameras. 'You're a natural,' Gabby told him.

'Is there anything you're not good at, Tom?' joked Vernon.

Tom grinned. He felt almost as comfortable in front of the cameras as he did in the pool. His mind flashed back to Rob's Elvis performances. Maybe he had got it from his dad?

Yes, TV was a definite possibility for the future.

But despite loving the bright lights and and cameras, Tom couldn't shake the feeling that was something missing. He was back in training, but somehow the excitement wasn't there. His competitive spirit had disappeared. He wasn't motivated like before. He didn't feel excited.

At just 18, had Tom achieved everything already? He had won gold at every major competition except the Olympics. Had he reached the peak of his potential as a diver?

Or... did he simply need a change? Did he need to shake things up?

Like the celebrities he was mentoring, did he need to push himself out of his comfort zone in order to move forward?

CHAPTER 22

THE FIREWORK

Tom had wished for change... and change is what he got.

He moved from Plymouth to London.

He started training at the London Aquatics Centre where he had won his bronze medal at London 2012.

He had a new coach, Jane Figueiredo.

He had a wonderful new boyfriend, Lance, whom he had met at an awards ceremony. Lance was an Oscar-winning screenwriter and Tom loved his passion, his brains and his sense of fun. Already they were dreaming of a future together. Marriage?

Children? Anything was possible! With Lance at his side, Tom was rediscovering his drive and determination. Suddenly life was exciting again. His will to win had returned.

Which was lucky, because the eyes of his new coach were firmly on the Rio Olympics in 2016 and gold medal glory. Andy Banks, and before him, Sam Grevett, had taught Tom everything he knew. Tom was so grateful for their hard work and dedication. But Jane's coaching was pushing Tom in new directions. She had inspired him with new confidence, new enthusiasm.

'I've been thinking about a new dive, Tom,' she told him. 'I think you should try a front three-and-a-half somersaults with a twist.'

Tom frowned in concentration as he imagined the movements, one after the other. Running along the board. Launching into the air. Spinning. Bursting out into a twist. Dropping down into the pool.

'Oh!' he exclaimed. 'I get it! No one will be expecting the twist!'

Tom's new coach, Jane, nodded. 'Exactly. It'll be a surprise. Like a firework exploding.'

'So who else has done the dive?' Tom asked. 'Can I watch a video?'

'There are no videos.' Jane grinned. 'No one has ever done it before. I saw a Russian circus performer doing it on YouTube. You'll be the first to do it as a diver!'

Tom's eyes widened, then a smile broke onto his face. The first person ever? That was exciting! 'And I won't have to do the Twister anymore?'

'No.' Jane smiled. She knew how much Tom hated the Twister. 'Okay, let's give it a go!'

Tom threw all his energy into learning the new dive. He started on the trampoline, perfecting the somersaults and twists. Learning a new dive was a slow and painstaking process, repeating every element over and over again until his body remembered it automatically – and his new coach was impressed by his patience and hard work.

After many hours on the trampoline, he moved

onto the three-metre board, putting the elements together in the right order under Jane's instruction.

From the three-metre board, he moved up to five metres, then to seven, then finally to the 10-metre platform. Tom knew it would take many months before the dive was ready. It wasn't about getting it right once. It was about getting it right every time.

And when it was ready, he wanted it to sparkle like the brightest firework, dazzling the judges and wowing the spectators.

Golden sunshine, a luminous turquoise sea, waving palm trees and distant blue mountains... Rio de Janeiro was Tom's idea of paradise. Right now, his mum and his boyfriend were sunning themselves on the Copacabana, gazing up at Sugarloaf Mountain and the giant statue of Christ the Redeemer. If only he could be enjoying it with them! Instead, he was training with his teammates, perfecting his dives for the preliminary round of the Olympic Games.

The Rio Olympics in 2016 were his third. Tom

was the strongest he had ever been, his dives were the most difficult. The hope and expectations on his shoulders had never been higher. But Tom was not going to let a bit of pressure get to him. He thrived under pressure. He ate up lunch. Bring it on! he thought to himself.

With Lance and Debs cheering noisily from the stands, Tom soared through the prelims in first place with an epic 571.85 points. The Firework was every bit as impressive as he and Jane had planned – it crackled with energy and excitement, and the crowd, and the judges, were delighted. Their hard work had paid off!

Tom couldn't wait to perform his showstopper dive in the final. He was dreaming of gold – and he knew Jane was too.

First, though, he must get through the semis.

Tom's first dive was an inward 3.5 somersault tuck. His performance was not as strong as in the prelims – but no matter. His points were good.

Up next was the Firework. No-one else in the

competition – or in the world – was doing this dive. It was unique and every time he performed it, he felt a buzz of pride.

But somehow instead of sparkling, his Firework fizzled. Just 54.00 points. From eighth on the leaderboard, Tom had sunk to seventeenth. Jane looked at him with worry. Was everything okay?

Tom smiled reassuringly at her. The Firework was just one dive. There were four more to go. Okay, it had been disappointing, but Tom had learned to let go of a bad dive and focus on the next one. He was confident he could claw back the points he needed to qualify for the final.

As Tom watched the other divers, he psyched himself for the next dive, an armstand. He always got good scores for this one.

But when the time came for him to climb the stairs and position himself at the end of the board, he found his heart was pounding. His legs were trembling – and when he landed in the water it was with a huge, whale-like splash.

Jane's head was in her hands. Was it really Tom she was watching? She had never seen him land like that, even in training. The judges awarded him just 42.75 points, half the score he had been hoping for.

Tom's mind was whirling. What was wrong with him? He was pretty sure his brain was saying the right things – but somehow his body wasn't doing them. He tried to push away his anxiety. I'm not giving up, he thought. Summoned his focus, he prepared himself for his fourth dive.

He scored 81.40. That was more like it!

His fifth dive was even better: 91.80.

To qualify for the final, Tom would need a phenomenal 101.00 points for his final dive. Poolside, Jane clenched her hands together nervously. Even for Tom, it would be a huge score... But Tom was capable of amazing things. Could he? Would he?

Hope turned to disappointment. As Tom crashed into the pool with a huge explosion of spray, she knew there was no chance.

Up in the stands, Lance and Debs looked at each other in shock.

And kicking back to the surface, Tom's face was a picture of gloom. A thousand thoughts were churning in his head. How had this happened? What had he done wrong?

Last on the leaderboard. No Olympic final.

Was it all over for Tom?

CHAPTER 23

MORE THAN DIVING

'Inexplicable,' said the papers the next morning.

No-one was more disappointed than Tom, of course. With his diving partner, Dan Goodfellow, he had won a bronze in the synchronised event. But standing on the podium, he had to force a smile onto his face. Inside he felt like his bubble had burst. He was overwhelmed by the feeling that he had let everyone down, his family, his teammates, his country. He felt ashamed, embarrassed.

'What went wrong?' asked Jane.

Tom could only shake his head. He was mystified. It hadn't been nerves and it wasn't an injury. He simply couldn't explain it.

'It was bad luck,' Lance told him. 'Plain and simple.'

But Tom couldn't be so easily comforted. For four years, he had put every ounce of his energy into training for Rio, and everything he had worked for had gone up in smoke. His confidence was in tatters.

'Do I even want to continue diving?' he asked Lance. 'Is it worth it?'

'Only you know the answer to that,' Lance replied gently.

Tom did know the answer. He *did* want to keep diving. But right now, he needed a break.

So together, Tom and Lance set off to do some travelling. From the top of the Statue of Liberty in New York, the pain of losing in Rio started to feel a bit less raw. Exploring the ancient Colosseum in Rome definitely helped Tom forget about his diving disappointment. And by the time Tom and Lance wandered along the River Seine in Paris, the

Olympics were a distant memory. In fact, Tom was starting to realise that maybe the setbacks were an opportunity. Diving had been his main focus since he was eight, his one passion. *But diving isn't everything*, he thought. Seeing the world with Lance had shown him that other things were important too. Tom knew he needed more balance in his life.

'You aren't filming this are you?' Lance glanced suspiciously at Tom's phone.

'Of course!' Tom grinned.

Vlogging helped him to find the fun in life, stopped him from getting too serious. His YouTube channel was filling up with videos of his travels, and he planned to film his training sessions and competitions too.

'I'm promoting diving,' he told Lance.

'You're promoting ice cream,' Lance laughed, daubing his boyfriend's nose with some icy vanilla.

It was true. They were both licking enormous ice creams as they walked.

'It's not even warm,' Tom said. 'Why are we

doing this?'

'I guess we just really love ice cream.'

Tom couldn't disagree with that.

After quality time with Lance, travels and relaxation, Tom found he was looking at the future with hope again. More than hope... excitement! He and Lance planned to marry in 2017, and when Tom wasn't training or competing, he threw himself into planning their wedding.

Jane and his teammates were delighted to see the smile back on Tom's face. And in the pool, Tom's happiness showed too. Just a few months before his wedding, he won gold at the World Championships in Budapest. After the pain of Rio, it felt fantastic to be enjoying a summer of celebration!

Having gone on to win gold with Dan in the synchro event at the 2018 Commonwealth Games in Australia, Tom took some time off. He had an important reason: the birth of his and Lance's son, Robbie Ray. Of all the amazing things that had happened in Tom's life so far, Robbie's birth was by far the most magical, better than any Olympic medal or World Championship victory. Looking into baby Robbie's eyes, Tom's heart did somersaults. The feeling of love and joy and pride was overwhelming. And after just a few weeks, swept up in the whirl of cuddles, nursery rhymes, nappy changes, midnight feeds, and more cuddles, neither Tom nor Lance could remember a time before Robbie.

Eventually Tom went back to training, leaving Lance to look after Robbie during the day. He worked harder than ever. Every moment with Robbie was precious, so every moment he had to spend away from him... well, Tom wanted to make it count.

As the 2019 competition season drew near, Tom knew that his next challenge would be the next run of international competitions. The thought of leaving Robbie Ray for weeks at a time filled Tom with sadness. First up was Montreal, 5,000 miles away, for the World Series.

'FaceTime me whenever you can,' Tom instructed Lance.

'I promise,' grinned Lance. 'You'll be seeing plenty of us.'

Seeing his son's beaming smile onscreen from his hotel room and the training area kept the smile on Tom's face. And in the pool his performance was sparkling. He leapt and flipped and twisted and somersaulted to a gold medal. If only his son could have seen him!

In February, Tom was back in Plymouth for the British National Championships and this time, Lance and Robbie would be there to watch.

'You're going to see Papa compete!' cooed Tom. They had decided early on that Tom would be 'Papa' and Lance would be 'Daddy'.

'And you're going to be well behaved for Daddy, aren't you, Robbie,' added Lance. 'No screaming the place down.'

'He'll be perfect!' said Tom.

But once he was up on the two-metre platform, Tom couldn't help listening for Robbie's cries. Happily... nothing! How well behaved his little son was being.

On the first day of the competition, Robbie and Lance, along with Nana Debs, watched Tom dive in the synchro, alongside his new diving partner, Matty Lee.

Success! Tom and Matty dived to victory, leading their nearest rivals by almost 60 points.

Day two was the individual event and once again, Lance, Debs and Robbie watched Tom take gold. Winning a gold medal in front of his young son... it didn't get much sweeter than that!

'You're my lucky charm, aren't you?' joked Tom, stroking Robbie's cheek.

And Tom's winning streak was set to continue. His most successful World Series yet came in 2019, with further medals in Gwangju and London, as well as being named the overall World Series champion. Everyone agreed – 12 years since he had first appeared in international competition, Tom Daley was one of the greatest divers of all time.

There was one question on everyone's mind though. Tom had won every other major championships – British, European, World – could he finally win an Olympic gold?

Following Beijing, Rio and London, the Olympic Games in Tokyo would be Tom's fourth. He was on the best form of his life. He had a fantastic coach. The support of a brilliant team. The love of an amazing family. Tom longed to make his young son, his husband and his mum proud. He longed to reward them, and his fans, for their support and loyalty.

Would Tokyo be his moment?

Cuddling his young son, his good luck charm, his very own 'Baby Daley', Tom hoped that it would be.

**TOM DALEY
HONOURS**

Olympic Medals

🏆 London 2012: Individual 10 m, Bronze

🏆 Rio 2016: 10 m Synchro, Bronze

World Championship Medals

🏆 Rome 2009: 10 m Platform, Gold

🏆 Kazan 2015: 10 m Platform, Bronze;
Mixed Team Event, Gold

🏆 Budapest 2017: 10 m Platform, Gold;
Mixed 3 m Synchro, Silver

🏆 Gwangju 2019: 10 m Synchro, Bronze

NAME:	**Thomas Daley**
DATE OF BIRTH:	**21 May 1994**
PLACE OF BIRTH:	**Plymouth, UK**
NATIONALITY:	**British**
SPORT:	**Diving**
Height:	**177 cm**
Main events:	**10 m Platform**
Club:	**Dive London**
Coach:	**Jane Figueiredo**

Olympic Medals

GOLD **0** SILVER **0** BRONZE **2**

World Championship Medals

GOLD **3** SILVER **1** BRONZE **2**